MART

YA
152.4
W

4

Wilkinson, Beth.
    Coping with jealousy / Beth Wilkinson. --
New York : Rosen Publ. Group, c1992.

    144 p. ; pc 7-12.

    SUMMARY: Defines jealousy, confronts its
destructive capabilities, and gives advice on
coping effectively with this negative
emotion.
    ISBN 0-8239-1516-6: $13.95

                         61504   MAY '93

    1. Jealousy.   I. Title.

                                            19
                            92-18567 /AC

Jealousy

Beth Wilkinson

THE ROSEN PUBLISHING GROUP, INC./NEW YORK

Published in 1992 by The Rosen Publishing Group, Inc.
29 East 21st Street, New York, NY 10010

Copyright 1992 by Beth Wilkinson

First Edition

Library of Congress Cataloging-in-Publication Data

Wilkinson, Beth.
    Coping with jealousy / Beth Wilkinson.—1st ed.
      p. cm.
    Includes bibliographical references and index.
    Summary: Defines jealousy, confronts its destructive capabilities. and gives advice on coping effectively with this negative emotion.
    ISBN 0-8239-1516-6
    1. Jealousy—Juvenile literature. [1. Jealousy.] I. Title.
BF575.J4W55 1992
152.4—dc20
                                        92-18567
                                         CIP

3 9082 05220254 9   AC

Manufactured in the United States of America

ABOUT THE AUTHOR ◇

Beth Wilkinson graduated from the University of Wyoming, Laramie. She has taught elementary school, high school reading and literature, and special education. Professional affiliations include membership in professional organizations and groups interested in literature, music, adult literacy, the young child, antiques, and art. Other interests are writing poetry and short stories, designing jewelry, and traveling. She spends her spare time near Sugar Loaf Mountain where she has a tree house, a line cabin, and acres for hiking. During summers and vacations her grown children visit her there.

Contents

1	What Is This Feeling Called Jealousy?	1
2	Where Does It All Start?	16
3	A Psychologist's Point of View	29
4	Rivalry and Recall	40
5	Winterset Home for Boys and Girls	56
6	Perceptions	70
7	Talk Shows	82
8	The Legacy	94
9	What It's All About	104
10	The Classroom	113
11	Trying to Stay Sane	126
	For Further Reading	138
	Index	141

CHAPTER 1

What Is This Feeling Called Jealousy?

J ealousy, like joy and misery, is a feeling experienced by everyone. Like breathing, it is seldom mentioned. Whereas happiness and unhappiness are easy to talk about, most people are unwilling to admit to such a distasteful emotion. Jealousy, born of fear, is a cluster of hurt, anger, and loss. It has divided families, been grounds for divorce, ruined careers, and brought down kingdoms. At one end of the scale it has caused violence and wanton cruelty. At the lighter end of the scale it has hurt feelings and alienated friends. Jealousy is a bitter feeling, and people who experience it often overreact and humiliate themselves.

"I can't believe my best friend telephoned Ned, and I'm furious," Penelope said. "Tibba and I have been friends since grade school, and now look what she's done."

"Exactly what *has* she done?" Grady asked.

"She's let me down, that's what. After all these years when we've traded clothes, joined the same clubs, and told each other our innermost secrets, she's betrayed me."

"Wait a minute," Grady said. "You quit dating Ned Hill three months ago. I'll admit it was tacky for her to call your old boyfriend, but the truth is, Pen, you're just plain jealous!"

For a moment Penelope stared at Grady in disbelief; then she began to laugh. "You know," she said, "you could be right, and frankly I'm embarrassed."

Penelope's story had a good ending once she took time to sort out her feelings. First of all, it was important for her to identify them. She needed to decide whether she was annoyed or angry with her friend or simply jealous of a situation that involved her former heartthrob. After all, a ten-year friendship with Tibba was not something to give up easily. Besides, Pen knew she had done some pretty dumb things, too, like borrowing her friend's favorite sweater and losing it. Another time she had promised to keep a secret and had let it slip. First Penelope took time out to cool off. Eventually, when she and Tibba did get together and the subject of Ned came up, she was able to talk calmly and explain how she had been hurt by the telephone call. However, Penelope never did actually say she had been jealous.

THE FEELINGS INVOLVED

Jealousy involves betrayal and feelings of insecurity and fear. Like a toothache, most emotions can be readily felt, but jealousy, that subtle emerald-eyed beast that most of us carry within ourselves, is unsettling and bewildering. Somehow it involves love and caring that seem threatened. Often we identify it as anger rather than jealousy, although anger is surely part of the package. It can also involve fear, pain, depression, and despair. Like a piece of a large puzzle, jealousy is a part of everyone's personality.

The belief that jealousy is immature and something we outgrow is wrong; it cannot be wished, wiped, or washed away. Unlike fries with a burger or pepperoni with a pizza, jealousy is not a desirable addition to anyone's personality. Its causes are an enigma, a mystery. As they grow older, most people become less self-centered and less possessive and *may* become less jealous, but not always. When our health is good and our self-esteem is high, it is possible that twinges of jealousy may decrease, but more likely they are only dormant. From infancy through the teenage years, young adulthood, middle age, and even in old age there will be times when jealousy arises. How well we learn to cope can make a big difference in our lives. Not learning to cope with jealousy can only make life's road bumpy and marked by difficult hurdles.

Definitions of Jealousy and Envy

The Random House Dictionary of the English Language defines jealousy as:

1. jealous resentment against a rival. a person enjoying success or advantage, or against another's success or advantage itself. 2. mental uneasiness from suspicion or fear

of rivalry, unfaithfulness, as in love or aims. 3. vigilance in maintaining or guarding something. 4. a jealous feeling, disposition, state, or mood.

The definition of envy is: a feeling of discontent or covetousness with regard to another's advantages, success, possessions.

The word jealousy has its earliest origins in a Greek word, *zelos*. *Zelos* implied a friendly rivalry. By the time the word found its way into English, however, it had acquired a more negative connotation.

According to the French *Académie* (1954 ed.), there are four kinds of envy; (1) the envy we feel because the profit is so great as to hurt our own; (2) the envy we feel because the welfare or profit for another has not happened to us; (3) the envy that makes us unwilling for any other to have an advantage that we desire or have wished for and could not get; and (4) the envy that makes us feel ourselves at a loss when others feel an advantage.

The Difference Between Jealousy and Envy

Envy can be combative and competitive. Envy is a feeling of discontent, usually with ill will, at another person's advantages or successes. An analogy for envy is: I want what you have and I don't want you to have it. In its mild form, envy could be expressed in a simple but sarcastic comment, "Her skirt is adorable but much too tight, and it would look ten times better on me."

Jealousy, sometimes called "love's curse," is resentment against a rival or a possible rival. It almost always involves love of another person or an object that symbolizes love.

When Rosa and Rico started going steady, everyone was happy. Everyone, that is, except Angie. Rico and Angie had been tight the year before, but it didn't work out and Angie returned his class ring. When Rosa had a birthday party for Rico at the Matador, Angie was furious. In a fit of rage she found Rosa's car near the restaurant and slashed the tires. Later, she couldn't explain her bizarre behavior; after all, it had been her decision to break off with Rico. Rosa had no trouble figuring out why Angie felt the need to do such a horrendous act. "She was jealous, of course," Rosa said. "She couldn't stand to see Rico happy and going with someone else."

Envious people live in a constant state of anxiety. Envy is a feeling or mood that can dominate one's thoughts, often becoming an obsession. This obsession can be with another person's money and possessions, such as cars and homes. Envy has been described as a painful or resentful awareness of an advantage enjoyed by another person, joined with a desire to possess the same advantage. Even the ability to do plain hard work can be a target of envy.

A Profile of Envy

Stella is a high school girl who is learning to deal with envy and readily admits that she seems to learn everything the hard way. "School is tough for me," she says, "but I find if I stick with it I can get passing grades. When I'm sidetracked, like being unhappy with a boyfriend or mad at my mom, it's impossible to concentrate. Maybe some of that happened last semester. I tried to keep the garbage out of my life, but it wasn't always possible. I was really envious when my younger sister made the honor roll. In fact, I ripped the lining in the leather fringe jacket Sis bought at a secondhand shop. It's weird looking, but it's her favorite. I like it too, and I saw it first at Bag Lady's, but that's another story. When I told her I was sorry that I did such a mean thing, she was cool. She said what she understands about me is that my brain tends to vapor-lock. Being envious is really a dumb thing to be."

The fact that Stella took responsibility for her action by apologizing to her sister is a plus. She is learning to handle her envy in a positive way. Stella recognized that the cause of her resentment was her sister's better grades. She realized that if she studied more she would be able to make better grades. She says her goal is to make the honor roll at least once during her high school career. This is a definite challenge, as she admits she'd much rather have fun, get involved in sports, and party.

Envy is different from jealousy, which involves love and possessions symbolizing love, and trying to get rid of a rival. In other words, envy has more to do with accomplishments and material things than with love. Both envy and jealousy are rooted in venom and at their most poisonous can be brutal. Envy is not as intense with most people. We all know that pickles, olives, grasshoppers, and peppermint are green. Perhaps if words came in colors, jealousy would be bright green and envy would be the color of pea soup. How one learns to cope with these emotions early on can determine how one manages them in later life.

Most dictionaries list covetousness as a synonym of envy or jealousy. To covet is to want what belongs to another; to wish for enviously. The Ten Commandments or Decalogue has an important place in the moral systems of Judaism, Christianity, and Islam. The Ten Commandments forbid coveting one's neighbor's property or wife. Different religions interpret these laws differently.

Jealousy and envy, like fraternal twins, are similar but not identical. Both involve discontent, usually with ill will, at seeing another person's advantages or success. Either one can dominate thoughts or feelings when constant images rerun in the mind. Dwelling on the things being envied or the object of jealousy depletes energy and consumes time.

For some reason, envy is often a more comfortable word to use when discussing the emotions of either envy or jealousy. Perhaps that is because the word jealousy has a harsh sound. Because most people use jealousy and envy interchangeably, it has become acceptable to define them as meaning the same.

KINDS OF JEALOUSY

There are several types of jealousy: sibling, social, professional, and sexual. Sibling means brother or sister; rivalry means competitive action between people, groups, or institutions.

Sibling Jealousy

Sibling rivalry means conflict between brothers, sisters, or brothers and sisters, each competing for a desired object, for affection or attention, or for the love they want or believe they are entitled to. Studies show that the younger the child, the easier it is for him or her to accept a newborn sibling. Nevertheless, many teenage boys and girls joyously welcome an infant brother or sister into the family. Sibling rivalry and jealousy are so closely woven together that it is often impossible to separate the two.

A Baby-Sitter's Story

"I've been a sitter since I was in middle school. This year I am taking a tenth-grade class called Childhood Development and Growth. It is a requirement, and taking baby-sitting jobs, getting to know and understand children, helps me with my schoolwork.

"One of my favorite 'jobs' is three-year-old David. His parents, Becki and Ray, tell me I do a fantastic job with David. I always read to him and tell him stories. He's a sweet little boy. At bedtime he never gives me a hard time. With David it's simple city— he loves to sing, so after I get him into his pajamas we sing until he falls asleep. When Becki and Ray told me they were expecting another baby, I was happy. For one thing, I knew I'd be able to earn more money. Becki and Ray were concerned that David might be jealous of a new baby. It happens. We talk a lot about sibling rivalry in my Childhood Development class. If parents aren't into child behavior they can really mess up. Becki's neighbor, Jean, said when her second baby was born they had all kinds of trouble because the first child was so jealous. Matthew, four at the time, once shoved his new baby brother under the sofa. Later, when the infant was sleeping, Matt covered the crib with blankets. Of course, he didn't realize the seriousness of his actions. He probably thought out of sight, out of mind. When Jean went for her six-week checkup, Matthew told the doctor to take the baby back. Of course, Becki laughed at all this, but I could see that it made her nervous. She told me that she and Ray spent evenings with David. They didn't go out of their way to entertain him, but they did put off evening chores so they could all be together. Usually David played with toys while Ray caught up on his reading and Becki sewed. They also talked to David about how they would need his help to rock the cradle, push the stroller, and even burp the new baby. We talked about this in Child Development, and everyone agreed that Ray and Becki were using excellent techniques.

"When Sarah was a month old, David had not shown many signs of jealousy. Recently, however, relatives visited from out of town. Everyone was thoughtful about bringing gifts for Sarah and something special for David too. The baby was admired and handed from one person to another. That's when David started acting crazy by making gross noises and throwing toys around. He was certainly trying to let everyone know he wanted his share of attention. David's grandfather said, 'Come here, David, I need hugs.' It had a very calming effect on David. The next day in class, we agreed that life is made easier for everyone when parents, friends, and family take time to show attention to older children when a new baby arrives."

Social Jealousy

Social jealousy takes different forms and can be intense. Adults may be vying for admission to the same club or trying to outdo each other in having a better car or a bigger house. Children, too, can be caught in the social jealousy trap. That's what happened to Jon. An especially insightful boy, Jon was able to resolve his jealousy with a happy ending.

Jon

"When I was a small boy, sandbox age, my best friend was Eric. Our dads had cut out on us, so we depended on each other; we were like brothers we were so close. When we were around seven, Saul moved into our neighborhood and Eric liked being around him. I felt terrible—I was jealous of Saul. I'd say, 'Eric, let's go to the park and not ask Saul.' Eric wouldn't agree. All I knew was that Saul was taking away my best friend, and I couldn't stand it. When I started second grade, Eric was in first and the darndest thing happened. Saul was in second grade, too, and we got to know each other. It's strange to think of a person as a foe and then become friends. The three of us, Eric, Saul, and I, have been buddies for years now. Once I got fed up with high school, life, and the world, and I left for Phoenix. After a while I missed my family, but mostly I missed Eric and Saul, so I returned home and went back to school. I believe that personal and professional jealousy is everywhere in our lives and one has to learn to deal with it. I'm glad I learned about it at a young age. I also know that most people are lucky to have one good friend, and I have two."

Professional Jealousy

Professional jealousy has to do with getting along in the workplace. It is important to have that ability as well as having job skills.

Jon was right when he said that personal and professional jealousy are everywhere in life. He has exceptional insight on the subject. When Jon returned from Arizona, he asked for his job back at the photocopy shop where he had been working part time. "They rehired me in spite of the fact that they had hired another part-time person. Jerry had some problems, but if he had ever learned to keep his mouth shut things would have been okay. He was jealous because they took me back and still considered me the senior clerk. I thought the boss was only being fair, and I appreciated that. I'd worked there year-round including vacations since my sophomore year. I'm sure that was taken into consideration. Jerry did a lot of petty things trying to make me look bad, and when that didn't work he got mad and walked out. I feel sorry about how things turned out, but the truth is, it's not my problem."

Doing the Right Thing

In the workplace, actions may speak louder than words when it comes to envy and jealousy. It is not only embarrassing but hurtful when a person is given an unexpected honor or recognition of a job well done and his or her coworkers fail to acknowledge it. It is also true that when one makes the team, sews a new outfit, has a story or a poem printed in the school paper, or wins ribbons at the fair, compliments are in order. To ignore these achievements with silence is bad manners. Not only that, but the indifference speaks loud and clear. Someone is jealous.

Sexual Jealousy

Sexual jealousy involves male and female relationships. It is a strong emotion, and in some people it explodes out of control. Jealousy is responsible for a high percentage of homicides in America. It is not unusual to read in the newspapers about crimes of passion, and it is a rare radio or TV newscast that does not mention murder as a result of a love triangle or an adulterous affair. Although the words jealous or jealousy are seldom mentioned, the implication is clear. As a rule it takes a less serious course than violence and murder, but all too often it does result in cutting remarks, tattling, gossipmongering, or acts of hurtful resentment. Careless talk and meddling are common forms of revenge when jealousy is involved.

Lost Love

For an age you may have had your eye on this cute girl or guy. You have passed notes in class, chatted on the phone, and talked in the halls at school. In the morning when you get dressed, you're particular about what you wear and how your hair looks. You want to make a good impression in case you see her or him "by pure accident." Everything is going great, and you're sure you'll have a date for the big dance that's coming up. Then all those hopes and dreams end with a heartbreaking crash. Maybe it was something simple that made you jealous. Perhaps in class you saw the person pass a note to someone else, and a chill went down your spine. You never stop to consider that the exchange may have been a petition, social studies notes, or even a recipe someone's mom asked to be delivered. All you know is how it looked. Every time you replay the scene in your mind, it triggers a terrible feeling. You remember the prom, which is not far off. Maybe your feeling is anger. You had your hopes up, and now they've been dashed by someone who has the same idea. That person, too, has dreams. It makes no difference; you are disappointed *and* angry, and if you think about it you'll realize it's all tied in with jealousy. How good or bad you are feeling about yourself may be a determining factor in how you handle the situation. You may be able to shrug it off and walk away, but not everyone can do that.

Sean and Tiffany

When Sean saw Tiffany talking to a tall fellow in art class, he was jealous. "Oh, well," he told a buddy, "I've heard she's easy, and I'm not interested in that kind of a girl." Later, still sullen, Sean told another friend about seeing Tiffany with "some guy that thinks he's hot" and again repeated his cutting remark about Tiff being "easy." If Sean had taken time to ask a few questions, he would have learned that Tiffany and Avery are cousins and were talking about the last family reunion they had attended. In jealous anger, Sean had said mean and spiteful things that could hurt the young girl's reputation. Maybe after giving it some thought he was sorry. However, there's no way to swallow spoken words. In some situations it may be wise to follow the motto, "Think twice and speak once."

In truth, no one goes through life without doing things that they later come to regret. That happened to Candy several years ago. Enough time has now passed for her to talk about her feelings and what happened when she discovered that her boyfriend was seeing someone else.

Candy

"Last year I had a boyfriend. He was very handsome,
like a Greek god. I thought the sun rose and set on
this beautiful man and oh, how I loved him. It's
sinful to think that much of anyone. When he started
to change toward me and stopped asking me out,
I knew something was terribly wrong. I asked him
what was going on, but he always said he had studying or work to do. I knew that was possible because
he wasn't living with his folks and was trying to finish
twelfth grade. So I decided to go to his place and
have a talk about why he didn't at least call. When I
walked into his trailer there was a really pretty girl
there. He acted surprised, and I remember that she
laughed at me. I resented that. I was so mad I
grabbed her long hair and dragged her out of the
place. I beat that poor girl half to death. Of course,
from then on, the guy wouldn't have anything to do
with me. When I think back I know I was jealous and
couldn't handle it. It's a wonder I didn't land in
prison."

Mending Fences

Sean, with his cutting remarks, tattling, and gossip did
not handle his jealousy well. Candy is aware that she
could have been charged with assault and battery and
hauled off to jail. Both came to realize that by seeking
revenge they "cut off their nose to spite their face." Certainly they owe apologies to the targets of their vindic-
tiveness. Possibly they will have the courage to do so
years from now. Apologizing is often called mending
fences. Phrases such as "eating crow" or "eating humble

pie" are sometimes used to describe apologizing for unacceptable behavior. Perhaps Sean or Candy will someday
write a letter or a note or make a phone call and ask
forgiveness for their actions. The courses their lives take,
the values they choose, and the insights they develop will
be determining factors in what their consciences dictate in
the future. At present, the ways they responded to their
jealousy indicate problems serious enough to warrant
seeking help from an understanding teacher or school
counselor.

Rule No. 1. Identify Your Feelings.

CHAPTER ◊ 2

Where Does It

All Start?

Psychology is the study of individual behavior, whereas social psychology is the study of how the individual behaves in a group. Behavioral science is the branch of learning that develop theories from observing humans or other living organisms such as rats, mice, or monkeys. People educated in this area are called social behaviorists.

The big question appears to be whether jealousy is inherited or learned. Emotions have been studied for decades without definite conclusions. What determines the feelings and intensity of jealousy in a person is like the question of which came first, the chicken or the egg. No one knows for certain. Another piece of the puzzle is the question of why some people handle jealousy more easily than others. Being able to cope seems to be tied up with self-esteem, life experiences, and courage—with wisdom tossed in.

Dan is in high school. He has lots of friends and an

after-school job at Pizza Hut, and he lives in a one-parent household. Last year he was drawn into a hurtful situation involving jealousy. It's hard to say why Dan was able to handle his situation so well; his only explanation is that he's too busy to dwell on junk.

Dan

"Listen, I know about jealousy, but what happened to me was almost funny. Last year when I was in the tenth grade I ran against a senior for student body president. I didn't actually expect to win because the other guy, Klaus, was not only two years older but he'd had a lot of experience dealing with school stuff—you know, chorus, varsity soccer, and drama club. Anyway, my friends encouraged me and I thought what the heck, it could be lots of fun making posters and name tags. It was fun writing slogans because my last name is Hand. That's me, Daniel J. Hand. GIVE DAN A HAND AND ELECT HIM PRES was one of our slogans. HAND HAND A HAND was another. Once a bunch of us got together and baked cookies shaped like a hand making an okay sign. The next day we passed them out at school. The whole thing was great fun and we all worked hard, but I lost the election anyway. Maybe I was jealous for a little while, but it was easy for me and the rest of the kids to rationalize that it was better for Klaus to win. After all, it was his last year in high school. Anyhow, I knew Klaus had won fair and square and I'd had a ball. Besides, I learned how to make darn good cookies.

"During assembly Klaus was congratulated on his election. Then, in front of 1,500 students, Klaus introduced me—get this—Klaus introduced me as the guy that didn't have any friends. It was weird. Everyone was stunned, and for at least thirty seconds the auditorium was totally silent. I was shocked, but I did manage to mumble congratulations of sorts. During those few seconds my mind flooded with the thought that the guy was actually jealous of me, a lowly tenth-grader, low man on the political totem pole. I guess what really bothered me was his saying that I didn't have any friends. Later, I heard that the school principal had a talk with him, and I can also say he had the guts to apologize. None of it really mattered then or now. I just think that jealousy hit old Klaus in the rear and that's his problem."

JEALOUSY IN LITERATURE

Jealousy is derived from the same word that gives us the word *zeal*. A zealot is a fanatic, or a person who shows zeal or fervor for a person, cause, or object. "Love is never without jealousy" is a 17th-century proverb. Hallowed texts such as the Torah, the Talmud, the Koran, and the Vedas—Jewish, Islamic, and Hindu writings— give instructions and advice regarding law, religion, culture, and politics. These sacred tomes contain stories, allegories, and parables of all aspects of life. They also explain what appalling damage can result from negative emotions. The Bible alone has thirty-eight references to jealousy. An explicit comment on jealousy can be found in Proverbs: "Wrath is cruel and anger is outrageous, but who is able to stand before envy?"

Othello is one of Shakespeare's many plays about the emotion. In 1887 it was made into a powerful opera, *Otello*, by the Italian composer Giuseppe Verdi. In the story the dire results of jealousy and envy are overwhelming suspicion, anger, and hate between two of the main characters, Iago and Othello. When Iago cunningly warns Othello against jealousy, the "green-ey'd monster," he undermines the Moor's trust in his wife. The end is remorse, murder, and overwhelming grief. Sophocles wrote plays around the passions of jealousy. Mythology, fable, and legend deal with the subject. Contemporary writers wrestle with it in fiction, magazine articles, biographies, and autobiographies. Jealousy is the subject of many TV situation comedies, miniseries, soap operas, and even commercials. In the last two decades romance novels with overwhelming conflicts of power, money, and jealousy have been among America's favorite books.

Jealousy is the motivation of a recent film, "Amadeus," about the Austrian composer Wolfgang Amadeus Mozart. Antonio Salieri, court composer to the Austrian emperor, hates the young Mozart, who had been a child prodigy and can compose and transcribe symphonies in his head. Salieri realizes that Mozart is a genius who writes masterpieces that will live forever. Violently envious, murderously jealous, he does everything he can to keep Mozart poor and unrecognized. Mozart dies at forty and is buried in a pauper's grave.

Contemporary poets often deal with the subject, and certainly children's books are crammed with themes of envy and jealousy. People of every age must be delighted to read poetry written especially for children in Shel Silverstein's *Where the Sidewalk Ends.* How siblings must grin as they read a poem that begins, "One sister for sale! One sister for sale! One crying and spying young sister for sale!" How can a brother or sister not giggle when running across the line, "Someone ate the baby," from a Silverstein poem aptly called "Dreadful."

In early times the hill people of the Missouri and Arkansas Ozark Mountains believed in omens, supersti-

tions, and signs. Many of them still do. Goldie Hawkins
said, "To tell if your true love is jealous, hold a buttercup
under his or her chin. If the yellow color of the flower is
reflected, so that the skin looks yellow, the person is
jealous." As she said this, Goldie gave a wink and showed
pretty dimples. For most people, folk tales are part of
their childhood. These stories tell of elves, hobgoblins,
dragons, and other magical creatures. They also address
feelings such as pity, honesty, greed, cruelty, hate,
tenderness, love, and jealousy. Cinderella was ill treated
by her jealous stepsisters, and Hansel and Gretel were
left in the woods at the instigation of their father's cruel
and jealous wife. "Snow White," written in the early
1800s by Jacob and Wilhelm Grimm, is almost everyone's
favorite fairy tale. Who can forget the queen's saying,

> "Mirror, Mirror on the wall"
> "Who's the fairest one of all?"

and the mirror replied:

> "Snow White is the fairest one of all."

The queen gasped and turned green with envy. Envy and
pride grew like weeds in her heart until she knew no
peace by day or by night.

LEARNING TO COPE WITH JEALOUSY

Jealousy and envy are like an illness except that there are
no pills marked J or E to cure you. Because we all feel the
emotion of jealousy sometime in our lives, we must work
at learning to control it. Not being able to take command
of our emotions can cause problems with physical as well

as mental health. Headaches, backaches, stomachaches, and numerous types of nervous behavior are only a few of the conditions that result from emotional upheaval. It is not easy to back away from anger, greed, hostility, resentment, jealousy, or envy. Learning to control these emotions can make life smoother. Learning to cope with negative feelings can make anyone happier.

It is rare, but now and then we learn from someone else's mistakes. Once in a while we learn by being told. Usually people learn by their own blunders, picking themselves up and starting over again. This contributes to personal growth only if the person does not repeat the same mistakes. Probably our best help in problem-solving is reading. Getting into the daily habit is helpful not only in learning and unearthing new information, but as a stress reducer, a form of great joy, the perfect hobby, and the basis for great conversations with friends.

A Noble Tale

Once upon a time a man wanted to give his son a special gift on graduation from high school. He wrote down instructions for living a good life, which pleased his son very much. The father decided to publish the rules, hoping they would help others. In 1991 a small, inexpensive paperback with a snazzy red plaid jacket went to press. Called *Life's Little Instruction Book,** it was written by H. Jackson Brown, Jr. and has sold half a million copies to date. It contains 511 numbered suggestions on how to make life easier. Number 319 advises: "Refrain from envy. It's the source of much unhappiness." Several of the

---

* Brown, H. Jackson, Jr. *Life's Little Instruction Book* (Nashville: Rutledge Hill Press, 1991).

maxims relate to jealousy. Try to recall them whenever you feel a nudge from the green-eyed monster:

> "Number 33. Treat everyone you meet like you want
>   to be treated.
> Number 38. Keep secrets.
> Number 81. Avoid sarcastic remarks.
> Number 300. Don't expect life to be fair.
> Number 141. Give yourself an hour to cool off before
>   responding to someone who has provoked you.
>   If it involves something really important, give
>   yourself overnight."

WHERE DOES IT ALL BEGIN?

What makes people tick has long been of interest to mankind. From early Greece to the Middle Ages, interest was shown in mental disorders. In the 18th and 19th centuries some reforms were made in the treatment of the mentally ill. In the early 20th century there was a movement dedicated to the prevention of mental diseases by guidance clinics and educational institutes. Psychoanalysis was developed, a technique practiced by medical doctors after advanced training. Psychiatrist, the correct name, or shrink, the slang term, is used to describe men and women skilled in this science. A psychologist is trained to counsel people and help them understand their behavior, but is not required to have a medical degree.

The Father of Psychoanalysis

Sigmund Freud (1856–1939) was trained as a neurologist but practiced psychiatry in the latter part of the nineteenth century. His method of treatment was called psychoanalysis, a word he coined. He is responsible for concepts such as *ego*, which means self; *id*, the unconscious part of the self; *psyche*, the mind, and *persona*, individuality. It is interesting to note that the theme of jealousy abounded in the great Freud's professional and personal life.

Anna Freud (1895–1982) was the sixth child of Sigmund and Martha Freud. Anna adored her father and while growing up was jealous of her mother and her mother's sister, Tante Minna, because of their places in his life. As an adult she gained her father's attention and affection with her dedicated work in the field of child development.

Dr. Freud's nickname for Anna as a child was Schwarzer Teufel, or "Black Devil." It sounds unkind in English, but it has a lighter connotation in German. *Schwarzer* means a person with dark eyes and hair. *Teufel* means devil, but in this context it implies "saucy," a description Freud often used.

Anna was jealous of her older sister, Sophie, and they had unending quarrels. When the girls were taught to knit, Sophie told Anna that she was not good at the task. Anna always remembered this comment. She became a compulsive knitter for the rest of her life, perhaps to prove a point. Sophie was pretty, and that, too, was hard for the plainer Anna to bear. Sophie was named after an attractive niece of a friend of her father's. Anna was named after the plain daughter of the same friend. Anna felt that her name was common whereas Sophie sounded sophisticated and charming. Freud tried to ease her jealousy by pointing out that Anna is a palindrome, a word that reads the same backward and forward. It is doubtful that this comforted the teenage girl. Perhaps she would have felt better had she known that the name Anna is from a Hebrew word meaning "grace."

When Anna's brothers, Ernst and Oliver, spent the summer with their father in Holland, Anna was filled with envy. Tension also continued between Sophie, her mother's favorite, and Anna. That may be why the family often separated during the summer, with everyone traveling in different directions. When away from her father, Anna wrote him many letters. In 1911, when Anna was sixteen, she wrote saying that she missed hearing him call her "Black Devil."

Melanie Klein

Melanie Klein (1882–1962) was a pioneer child psychoanalyst who invented play therapy. This skill we often see used in documentaries or news reports when a psychologist is trying to learn the truth in cases of child abuse. Klein's analysis of child development has been of key importance to the psychoanalytic theory of personality development. Klein believed that envy starts in the cradle. Among many findings, she established that learning to give and receive love in infancy leads to higher self-esteem in adult life. Deprivation of love, comfort, and affection at birth and in infancy can cripple the development of the ego, the self. This can result in a personality stunted by envy, incapable of generosity and love in the growing years and later life.

Melanie Klein's work, psychoanalysis, investigates the unconscious thought processes and is used in treating psychoneuroses. Klein also suggested that guilt is the beginning of turning away from envy and hatred. Shame at our behavior often removes us from the person we envy; keeping a distance seems to be important.

THE PRELUDE

When a probe is inserted into a mother's womb, the fetus moves. Pregnant women often talk to their abdomen intending to soothe their baby. When a child is born it gives a lusty cry signaling its arrival. An infant also is able to feel, see, hear, and smell. At its very beginning it is conscious of being dry or wet, comfortable or uncomfortable. An infant readily responds to loud noises, its eyes follow objects, and it hungrily gobbles nourishment. It is aware of physical sensations and gratifications but has not yet developed an emotional system. As it grows, the infant becomes more and more aware of its surroundings and feelings and the feelings of others. It also becomes aware of what it wants, what it doesn't want, and what are perceived to be limits. In the first five years of life the human acquires an incredible amount of knowledge and skill. Because of development, adolescence is a time when doubts set in. It is the time for exploration and questioning.

Envy and jealousy are unpleasant and negative emotions, whereas admiration and contentment are positive emotions. Emotions are considered physical responses in which changes can be noted in pulse rate, body temperature, and breathing. Fear, love, and anger are usually considered the primary emotional responses. These feelings may be aroused directly or triggered through memory.

Emotions are also part of the personality, and we all have predispositions or inherited tendencies to good and bad, mild and strong, simple and complicated behavior. Emotional expression varies in different cultures, suggesting that emotion is partly learned.

No one knows when a person becomes conscious of

positive or negative feelings. Certainly one realizes very early in life when one is wet or dry, happy or sad, comfortable or uncomfortable. It is not until one becomes aware of other people's reactions, however, that one begins to learn to deal with emotions.

Aunt Nancy and Tweet

Nancy is thirteen years old and comes from a large family. When her eldest sister and brother-in-law, Madge and Lance Newhart, had their second child, grandparents, aunts, uncles, and cousins went to the Newharts' home to welcome the new arrival. It was a great party with a wonderful supper including angel food cake and ice cream. Nancy had looked forward to it and to seeing her two-year-old niece, Tweet.

As a gift, Nancy brought her niece an anatomically correct doll, which Tweet hugged and immediately named Mark, after her new brother. It was a happy time for everyone, and Tweet smiled as she sat with her teenage aunt. People said nice things about little Marky, but they also said lovely things to Tweet. When it was Tweet's turn to hold her new brother, Aunt Nancy helped with the soft blue blanket. Together, the teenager and the two-year-old cooed, giggled, and patted the new baby.

Then a dreadful thing happened. The baby began to cry and Tweet's mother picked it up and put its mouth to her breast. Anger clouded Tweet's face. "Mine," she cried. "My nummies." Everyone laughed and told Tweet she was a big girl now, much too big to be nursing.

Nancy knew that it had only been in the last few months that Tweet had been eating solid food. Many times, after school, Nancy had hurried to Madge's and had helped feed her. This was always special because all of Nancy's younger siblings were brothers. In fact, Nancy had nicknamed the little girl Tweet after a favorite cartoon character. Nancy knew that until recently Tweet had been allowed to nurse at bedtime.

Now people kept telling the little girl to calm down and act like a big sister. The more they scolded, the more furious Tweet became. She sobbed, kicked, and hiccupped as people shook their heads and frowned. "Straighten up," a relative cautioned. "For shame," another admonished. "Uh-oh," said still another, "our little Tweet is jealous." Finally Nancy coaxed her to another room and soothed her with calming words. "I know, Tweetybird," Nancy said, "not long ago I was given a new baby brother, too. It's not easy when everyone seems to give priority to something that looks like a squashed marshmallow." She rocked the little girl and told her stories of how she had felt when a new baby came along. Although Tweet did not understand her aunt's words, she did understand the tone and calmed down. Eventually she wanted to return to the family party and enjoy the ice cream and cake.

Nancy knew that it would take a while for Tweet to forget that she had been forever denied her mother's milk, but with time that, too, would be resolved. Nancy also knew that Tweet had experienced her first, but not last, feeling of jealousy. It is possible that Nancy's kindness and understanding were a gift to her niece. Subconsciously, it may have given Tweet the first tool for coping with jealousy: When faced with jealousy, try to stay calm.

When asked, Dan Hand made up several maxims for being jealous or provoking jealousy. Among them; KEEP COOL and COMPOSURE COUNTS.

Rule No. 2. Stay Calm.

CHAPTER 3

A Psychologist's
Point of View

Darrell W. Pendley is a practicing school psychologist, educational consultant, and stress management counselor. Asked to describe his professional philosophy of the human condition, Dr. Pendley says: "This is a tough one . . . especially in only a few words. I would say my professional and personal philosophy in regard to human need is like that expressed by author William Glasser. We all have the need to love and be loved and to feel we are worthwhile to ourselves and others. These are the paramount necessities for everyone, young or old.

"As for what I believe cultivates most feelings of jealousy, I suspect it is motivated by: (1) someone's gaining possession or getting the attention of someone that we consider ours, such as a boyfriend, girlfriend, or relative; (2) someone's owning more material items of monetary value; a sports car or a truck with mag wheels could be examples; (3) someone's having physical or mental skills or accomplishments that we long to possess; being a sports star or getting straight As; and (4) physical attractiveness; when we know another person looks better than we, a brother or sister that everyone in the family calls 'the good looking one'."

Ideally parents teach a child at an early age how to cope with jealousy. If that is not possible, the person overwhelmed by the emotion must work at resolving the problem. This is no small challenge. The key is first to recognize that something is amiss and then learn what our needs are and how to fulfill them. That is what growing up is all about.

QUESTIONS AND ANSWERS

To understand the feelings of jealousy, a question and answer interview with Dr. Pendley seems in order. In the following dialog the Q identifies the interviewer, and the A identifies Dr. Pendley's answers.

Q: When does jealousy begin?
A: Jealousy probably begins in infancy with a basis in self-concept and self-esteem. Important emotions develop as a child bonds with its mother. Bonding is the crucial attachment of a child to a parent figure. Long before children can put words to the feelings they may experience, they present behavior patterns. Some of these can be interpreted as pleasure, contentment, rejection, and jealousy. The infant does not consciously think or process these feelings. He or she merely experiences them.

I believe the mechanisms that give rise to emotions are present within us before we are actually born. The question of when jealousy begins is debatable. Infants present behaviors that are very selfish, which can be a part of jealousy, but this is done more out of self-centeredness. It is typical of that developmental stage. Jealousy does not seem apparent until the child is a bit older . . . two to three years of age. Selfishness and jealousy can be close emotions but are distinctly different. I know that you've heard a mom or dad admonish, "Now Johnny or Jenny, don't be selfish." Parents are not always good at explaining the feelings and the unpleasant end results of jealousy.

Q: Around what age is a person aware of this emotion?

A: A young child begins to realize that he or she is capable of experiencing different kinds of emotions. It begins at approximately three years of age. Children at this age become aware of something that adults call jealousy, and their understanding of what are called "feelings" is limited. Emotions in children are intense no matter what the age. They don't inhibit or cover up moods and outlooks as adults do; they express them: happy or unhappy, acceptable or unacceptable.

To learn to deal with jealousy, children must understand what has happened to give them the feeling they refer to as bad. As youngsters become teenagers they reassess their thoughts and feelings about life, friends, and the world around them. In adolescence everyone has to reevaluate many things because of physical development and social expectations. As teenagers become adults, hormones cut loose in the body and they begin to feel and think differently.

Q: Are certain nationalities or groups of people more prone to jealousy than others?

A: It does seem that jealous behavior is more pronounced in some societies than in others. This may be due to cultural beliefs that result in a more pronounced type of behavior. All groups of people have basic emotions such as love, hate, guilt, and anger, including envy and jealousy. Even in societies where these emotions appear to be accepted, some people learn to manage negative feelings more easily than others. In a society where the adults model extremely jealous behavior, the youngsters are more likely to present the same display of jealous behaviors.

　　People talk about "hot-blooded" in reference to nationalities that show expressive emotions, usually in romantic situations. Consequently, certain groups may have the reputation of being prone to jealousy and envy. However, I suspect jealousy is much more a learned than a hereditary trait.

Q: Is jealousy a more intense emotion for teenagers than other age groups?

A: Let's just say it's intense for the teenagers. Certainly it often seems to be overwhelming for the young person experiencing it. If young children were able to discuss their emotions as teens do, they would say they experience jealousy every bit as intensely as adolescents. Have you ever watched a three-year-old throw a tantrum? It is one way the young child deals with feelings of jealousy. The simple difference is that the teen has usually learned how to manage the enormous weight of negative behavior.

Another important factor is the world we live in. Society spends millions of dollars telling teenage boys and girls that they must have designer clothing and shoes, TV games, and sports cars in order to count. Young people often believe it and feel inadequate if they don't have what the ads pitch and famous people endorse. When other teens have what is considered essential by their peers, it easily arouses and fosters jealousy.

The teen years are a time when the body, mind, and spirit all undergo significant changes. Hormones released in the body allow feelings to arise that are completely different from any that the young person has previously experienced. An awakening of sexual energies, in particular, gives rise to a whole new category of feelings. It lends an intensity to jealousy. When dropped by a girlfriend or boyfriend, the teenager's feelings include jealousy as well as pride, anger, annoyance, and disgust. In today's world young people are encouraged to think and feel differently—be their own person, do their own thing. This makes all feelings seem more significant. Thus, the actions that teens sometimes choose in dealing with their problems may have a more serious aftermath. This might be because of the differences in consequence for the adolescent versus the child. Keep in mind that a cookie or a lollipop can soothe hurt feelings in a little person, but cookies and lollies don't work with young adults. That's when a lot of kids get into trouble: when they resort to adverse substitutes to solve problems.

Q: What are the feelings of jealousy?

A: Trying to describe the feelings of jealousy is like trying to explain the feelings of love—complicated. The unabridged dictionary has as many as forty definitions for love, but not one does justice to the feelings most people experience when they are "in love." Unlike the elation of love, everyone who has experienced jealousy is aware of feeling something unpleasant. It's a combination of being illogical, confused, and frustrated, plus feelings of hatred and guilt.

As humans we are first and foremost emotional beings. All our lives we go around feeling and expressing emotions. Too often we are told not to feel this or express that, yet everything we experience has an emotional component. Memories and longings invariably spark sentiments, good and bad. Ironically some people enjoy the mood or frame of mind jealousy puts them in. Also, neurotic hang-ups seem to be a way of life for a lot of Americans.

Q: What are the best coping skills to fend off jealousy?

A: Prevention is always the best medicine. Focusing on developing positive and confident feelings about oneself and one's abilities is worth the effort. Knowing and accepting our strengths and weaknesses allows us to be able to handle jealous situations when they arise.

Everyone needs to understand his own importance in the world. When we learn to like ourselves and know our strengths, life becomes easier. When we acknowledge our weaknesses and work at strengthening them, jealousy becomes less of a problem. Understanding emotions and learning to deal with them at an early age helps build tenacity, a wonderful character trait in anyone.

Q: How can we discourage jealousy in other people?

A: No matter what we do or how hard we try, there will be times when other people will be jealous. Keep in mind that jealousy is a strong emotion and it is often used to manipulate others—*to get people to do things they might otherwise be reluctant to do.* There are those who want to dominate and control, and manipulation is a way they do that. Acting jealous, making someone pay a price, is not uncommon behavior in many boy/girl/love relationships. For example, Jack forgot to call Jessie last evening, so Jessie gives him the cold shoulder all day. When she sees him in class or in the hallways, Jessie refuses to speak. This is her way of making him pay because he forgot to phone her. She justifies her bad behavior by telling herself that he probably called someone else, but in her heart she knows that is not true. Plain and simple, she is angry because Jack is not giving her the attention she demands. Pretending to be jealous makes her feel good and gives her the power to manipulate Jack. Chances are he will believe that she is crushed because she thinks he telephoned someone else. Her show of jealousy will make him feel wanted, needed, and important—for a while. If he's smart, he'll figure out that Jess is actually a schemer. He'll call, all right—someone else.

The best way to understand jealousy is to pretend one is dealing with the problem in oneself. To discourage jealousy, it helps to present oneself

as confident and up-front. I would say that would
be the first step. A second step might be com-
munication, talking it out. That way the subject
can interact with the jealous person in a positive
manner. These two suggestions certainly can
model for the covetous or envious person, who
can also deal with the problem in an honest,
straightforward way. After that it is up to the
jealous person to begin coping with his or her
feelings.

Q: Is jealousy a sign of real love?

A: Genuine love does not include jealousy. A relationship is doomed to tough times when one
person is so insecure that he or she cannot allow
the other to have any acquaintances, chums, or
buddies of the opposite sex. A person who understands love and experiences love does not exhibit
jealousy. To be able to love another person, you
must first be able to love yourself. If you can't
love yourself, but instead have strong feelings of
jealousy, all you have to offer another person is
an unhealthy relationship. Jealousy ruins more
relationships and friendships than any other
emotion.

Q: Explain sibling jealousy?

A: This is often referred to as sibling rivalry. When
brothers and sisters begin to feel they are not
treated equally by their parents or other people
in their lives, they often become angry and jealous. Sibling rivalry involves one child's receiving
attention, emotional support, or material objects
the other child feels he or she deserves. Numerous books have been written on the subject of
sibling interactions and how the number of

siblings and their ordinal position, or birth order, can affect behavior. When a child perceives a parent as favoring another sib, it is natural that he or she will object in some way. Jealousy is understandable when one feels that there isn't enough love to go around.

Q: Can a family avoid the problems of sibling jealousy?

A: Yes. Again the basis lies in being able to love and nurture all members of the family unconditionally and with fairness. That is not always easy. Becoming adults does not automatically make us able to deal effectively with emotions. It's interesting that in some families where the parents show extreme jealousy, the children have learned to deal effectively with their own jealous feelings. They have rejected that particular part of their parents' behavior. It is not unlike some children of alcoholics who never drink; the behavior they have observed is so repugnant that they renounce alcohol completely. Of course, this is more unusual than usual. After all, we learn from our parents. They are our very first teachers.

Keep in mind that the fact that your parents have never learned to handle jealousy doesn't mean you can't. With work and determination you can learn to cope with jealousy at any age. All humans throughout their lives are capable of "changing for the better."

Q: Why isn't jealousy one of the deadly sins?

A: The seven deadly sins are lust, anger, pride, sloth, avarice, gluttony, *and* envy. First of all, let's simplify the definitions of the seven deadly sins. Pride is assumption of personal superiority. *Lust* concerns desire and passion. I guess everyone understands the meaning of *anger*, but let me say that anger mirrors jealousy. *Sloth* means laziness, unconcern, and even being too laid back. *Avarice* is synonymous with greed and selfishness, but it also can mean covetousness. Another word for covetousness could be lust. *Envy* and jealousy are also synonymous. *Gluttony* is overindulgence or, more simply, making a pig of oneself. No matter how you look at it, all of the seven deadly sins are forms of self-indulgence. They all reflect one another in some way.

I certainly agree that these seven traits or passions are deadly. However, I can add several undesirable traits. The one that comes immediately to mind is *shunning*—not speaking to people, snubbing them. Perhaps this comes under pride, but I don't think so. When you are shunned you feel terrible. To be avoided or ostracized by groups is horrible for anyone. Discrimination and shunning are certainly twin emotions. Still, being shunned is better than being the shunner, just as being discriminated against may be a healthier situation than being a bigot. Somehow it all ties in with jealousy. Like guilt and anger, jealousy is an emotion that is part of us and something with which we all must learn to cope.

Q: What advice would you to give someone who is having trouble coping with jealousy?

A: My advice would be to seek help from a teacher, a school counselor, or a psychologist. Never be afraid to talk over your problems with someone you trust. Above all, realize that you have taken a giant step by admitting that there is a problem.

Something to Think About

Role-playing or thinking about how you would handle a jealousy-producing situation can help. Some people call this preplaying: rerunning the past before the window of your mind. For example, professional athletes are encouraged to review mistakes of a previous game. Then in a quiet, calm, relaxed state they visualize successful moves in an upcoming event. They do this over and over, seeing themselves victorious as they complete the exercise. This thought process is an effective tool in many situations, including dealing with jealousy. Why not plan ahead for the next time when you could be faced with the problem? Sit quietly and imagine yourself in a situation where you are bruised and in pain because of jealousy. In your mind see yourself poised, positive, and looking your best. You are calm, collected, and completely without fear. You are able to speak without overreacting or being nervous. The next time you are confronted with the Big J, recall your fearless behavior in that fantasy. Become the same strong person you visualized. You will be better able to cope with an unpleasant situation. The end result will have been well worth while.

Rule No. 3. Know That Learned Behavior Can Be Unlearned.

CHAPTER ◇ 4

Rivalry and Recall

R ivalry between siblings is part of life. The give and take of brothers and sisters and dealing with the resulting behavior are important. Siblings, unlike parents in this age of high divorce rates, are generally friends for life. Close adult relationships run smoother when the skills of coping with competition are learned in early childhood.

"Little Willie" is a pertinent bit of doggerel:

> Little Willie began to squall
> When Sister Nell, so sweet and small,
> Was given presents all mighty fine.
> He smacked her good and cried, "That's mine!"
> —*Beth Wilkinson*

Obviously there was sibling rivalry between Little Willie and Sister Nell. Evidence of violence in the rhyme is probably more truth than poetry. Unfortunately, it's that way in many families.

Chad

"Man," Chad says, "when my sister and I were kids it was war, and I mean all-out war. Carrie and I fought so much that we didn't get to know each other until last year when we started high school. Now we're friends . . . really tight." Chad's story is a familiar one. So are the woeful words of his older married sister, Bette. "I can't understand why my children are always fighting," she says. "We have at least six Little Tyke toys with wheels. If one child has the wagon, the other kid gets off the trike and demands it. They're constantly taunting each other, too. 'Look,' my daughter will say to her brother, 'I've got your Candy Land game.' Of course, that sends him into a frenzy."

"Yeah," Chad agrees, "that's what happens, and that's exactly how Carrie and I acted when we were little. We were really mean and jealous of each other. I'm sorry about that. We both try to talk to Bette's kids about it. Sometimes it even works, at least for a while, then boom, one will do something to drive the other one crazy. Maybe this kind of weird behavior is inherited. I don't know. What I do know is that being jealous, fighting about mundane things, and trying to do paybacks is a rotten way to spend your life. There's nothing Carrie wouldn't do for me and nothing I wouldn't do for her. We respect each other. We both hope Bette's kids catch on before they get to high school, because if they don't change they're going to waste a lot of time."

JOYFUL BUT JEALOUS

We are living in a time of change. In earlier days children were seen and not heard. Old-fashioned discipline included a smack on the bottom for a naughty child. In the past, spanking, ignoring, or refusing to acknowledge a disobedient child was a common way of dealing with children. Boys and girls were expected to behave in a prescribed manner. Less consideration and thought were given to how they might feel. A certain way of behaving was expected from sisters, brothers, moms, dads, teachers, and preachers.

When asked, a group of first-graders discussed what happened after a new baby arrived in the family. In describing their feelings upon seeing the baby for the first time, they used words like happy, glad, sparked, excited, and proud. When asked how they felt later, when the newness had worn off, some of the children became noticeably anxious.

Ahmed: I said some bad words about my baby brother, and Mom grounded me for two days.

Lily: For a while I got angry because Mom and Dad spent less time with me.

Xing: I would cry because the baby kept crying.

Lily: I told Dad, "You've got to take care of me, too."

Ahmed: I told the baby, "I don't like you, I just put up with you."

Xing: Sometimes I wish I was a baby.

Lily: I felt so bad. My new little sister got all the presents. It's not fair.

Ahmed: All I hear is: "Wait a minute, be quiet, and
   be careful." I get tired of that.
Xing: I *never* cried when I was a baby.
Lily: I'd like some presents—lots of them.
Ahmed: They always say, "Don't nag. Don't tease."

The wonderful part of young children's nature is that
they are truth-tellers. Young children call it as they see it.
The first-graders were honest in describing their feelings
about their sibling's arrival. They agreed about what made
their parents seem indifferent. They admitted that with
less sleep parents become tired, and it's easy to be cross
with active and demanding older children. Maurice said,
"Mom and Dad have to ignore me some of the time
because a new baby takes a lot of time crying and wetting
its pants."

Talking with first-graders is fun. At ages six and seven
they are uninhibited, always have big smiles, and make
gifts of blue-and-purple dinosaur pictures. When told that
a brother or sister is called a sibling, they laughed. First-
graders laugh a lot. "When I first heard that word, you
know, sibling, I thought it was probably a fish," Maurice
said. This was such a good joke that he fell out of his desk
chair.

When the children were asked if they could fast-forward
their lives, like a favorite video, and become teenagers,
they answered, "Piece of cake." The big question: When
you and your siblings are teenagers, how will you treat
one another? They agreed they would certainly be friends
and would play, laugh, watch TV, swim, and eat at
McDonald's. Their lives together as teenagers would also
include going to Disneyland, reading, borrowing the car,
making sandwiches, and helping with homework. If they

get angry with each other they will punch, kick, hit, and put KEEP OUT signs on their bedroom door. They also responded with ideas like: "When my sister is in junior high and I'm in senior high we'll talk a lot on the phone." "We'll ride bikes together and go on picnics." "I don't know if I'll like my sister when she's older, but I'll get along with my brother because we're both boys."

These children were perceptive and honest about their future relationships and obviously put thought into how they will feel about their siblings when they become teens. With good fortune their plans for enjoying one another's company will become reality.

PARENTS

Parents get tired. They run out of energy, drive, and enthusiasm. Sometimes they become disheartened. They have tried everything and are out of ideas of what to do about the disruption of routine in the household. Mothers and fathers sometimes are so overwhelmed by their children's scrapping, arguing, and threatening one another that they simply give up. Sometimes it is easier to accept the situation than to try to deal with it.

Reverting to "Careless Willie," it is obvious that there was sibling rivalry between Willie and his sister. It is also clear that their mother gave up trying to cope with the bizarre behavior of Willie and Nell:

> Willie with a taste for gore
> Nailed his sister to the door.
> Mother said, with humor quaint:
> "Now, Willie dear, don't scratch the paint."

> —*Anonymous*

Tony

Tony Tartelli has an interesting history. He is a third-generation American. His great-grandfather immigrated to the United States in the early 1930s. He brought his young family from Italy because he recognized war clouds on the horizon. First he sold fruits and vegetables from a pushcart. Next he owned a stall, then a small shop where he sold produce. Eventually he was able to buy a warehouse where he began a wholesale business, selling fruits and vegetables to retail grocery stores. Now, years later, Tony lives with his parents on the third floor of that same warehouse. Tony's great-grandfather died a long time ago, and the pushcart, stall, and shop are things of the past. Fruits and vegetables are now trucked out of the warehouse to supermarkets in all parts of the state. Tony, the oldest in a family of several boys, is expected to work part time, as all the sons in the Tartelli family have done for generations.

Tony seems to be handling his unique situation well. It is also important to note that he has parents in whom he can confide. Not everyone is so lucky. Best of all, Tony Tartelli is able to laugh at himself.

"I go to an inner-city school and feel proud that my high school is drug-free. My great-grandfather's name was Antonio; Grandpa was also Antonio but changed his name to Anthony. My dad is also Anthony. We are four generations of men named Tony. When I have a boy, I'm going to name him Popeye. That's a joke. Ma says I joke around too much.

"At our place, the Tartelli Warehouse, the first floor is where business is done. The second floor is for food storage, walk-in refrigerators and freezers, that sort of thing. The third floor is an apartment where my family live. The fourth floor was a play area for my brothers and me, but since I've gotten older and work I don't have a lot of time to get up there. We all get along okay most of the time. Sometimes I get tired of my younger brothers. They're still too little to work in the business. They get to do stuff I didn't get to do when I was younger. Carlo, Vinny, and Benito all have Nintendo games. In fact, they have just about anything you can think of that's electronic. I feel resentful. Mostly, because I work, I have to buy any games or equipment I want. Pop told me that when I was little he and Ma didn't have the kind of money they are making now. As a matter of fact, that's the way it seems with most kids from big families. It's the pits; the oldest always gets the short end of the stick. I guess being mad about it is a form of jealousy. On the other hand, though, my little brothers always beg me to take them to the park so we can throw the ball around. They think it's cool to be seen with me because I'm in high school. Hey, maybe the little reptiles are jealous of me! Maybe it's some kind of a trade-off.

FAMILIES

It is true that in large families the older children often do not have as much as the younger brothers and sisters. In this era the cost of living is high. The expectations of children and their parents are often greater than they were in earlier times. In single-parent families or families where both parents work there is rarely time to give the attention and affection that everyone needs, wants, and demands. Stress is greater in families because of the circumstances that they face. The problems of the high divorce rate, teenage pregnancy, AIDS, and alcohol and drug abuse cause anxiety and apprehension for most families. If these situations are not dealt with in a reasonable manner, anger, envy, jealousy, and fear take over.

Tesa

Tesa is not laughing. She not only has feelings of jealousy, envy, and anger but despair. Tesa, like Tony Tartelli, is from a large family. Unlike Tony, Tesa is the youngest. This is her last year in high school, and she has always planned to go to college. Tesa's older brother and sister graduated from a university many years ago. Their parents have required their children to be responsible for half of their tuition and all the costs of textbooks. The parents pay dorm fees, which include most meals in the cafeteria, and the remaining half of tuition. Family rules include working part time, saving money, and getting good grades. Tesa did these things just as her older brother and sister had done. During the school year she has done baby-sitting, and in the summer she works at McDonald's.

For almost four years at Thomas Jefferson High, Tesa has saved what she considers tons of money. She has also worked hard to keep up her grades. Only recently has she learned about the escalating costs of college—that by the time she graduates from Jefferson tuition fees will have gone up seven percent. There's no way that without financial help she'll be able to go beyond her sophomore year. Her older sister suggested that she apply for a student loan.

"After all," she told Tesa, "Bro and I got loans, and there's no reason you can't."

When Tesa inquired at the financial aid office at college she couldn't believe her ears. Since her brother and sister had graduated, her father had advanced in his company, with equivalent salary increases. His income is now considerably more than when Tesa's sister started college. Tesa is caught in a Catch 22 situation: Her father earns too much for her to be considered for a loan.

Even though times have changed, Tesa's parents won't help her financially. After all, they say, the other two kids got through school on their own for the most part. It wouldn't be fair.

Says Tesa, "I'm furious. I'm mad at my folks and everyone else in the world for making things so bad for me. I can't carry out the plans I've had since I can remember. I am also jealous that my brother and sister were able to go to college, graduate, and get good jobs. I don't see that happening to me."

Not everyone has structured parents, at least not as structured as Tesa's parents. They think their daughter will do all right in dealing with her situation, but it may take a while. Although her options are few, they think Tesa needs to figure it out. Some possible answers: (1) She may be able to get a better-paying part-time job after a couple years of college; (2) her older siblings may give or lend her money; (3) in the next few years university budgets may loosen up, enabling them to offer cheaper tuition; or (4) Tesa could drop out of college for a few years, work at a full-time job, and go back to school as a reentry student. At that point, she could qualify for a loan on her income rather than her father's.

Tesa's parents are also assuming that their daughter has the intelligence, insight, and understanding to cope with her jealousy and anger. Unfortunately, the family of our friend "Silly Willie" does not have the same trust and expectations.

> Willie with his eyes of green
> Was always jealous, always mean.
> Thus his family lost all hope
> That their Willie'd ever cope.
> —*Beth Wilkinson*

FAMILY VIOLENCE

Everything we learn before the age of five has an impact on the rest of our lives. People who have positive experiences during childhood develop confidence and self-respect. They are less prone to overreact in difficult situations because they are better equipped to handle their emotions in a positive fashion.

Jealousy all too often breeds brutality. A common thread in society seems to be the horror of child abuse. Each year hundreds of children are killed by parents, baby-sitters, relatives, and strangers. The brutalization of a child may come from extreme anger, resentment, or jealousy. Years ago Casey Cantrell's new stepmother had all of those feelings.

Casey

Casey is seventeen and says he has an okay home life. He calls his stepmother by her first name, Jill, and says he gets along better with her than with his father. "Jill is cool and easy to talk with," he says. "When I want to go someplace or stay out late, I talk to her. She's more likely to give me the go-ahead than Dad. She also gives me money if she thinks I need it."

Casey Cantrell's life was not always so normal. "There were things that made Jill's life and my life really bad," he says. "Once she was accused of breaking my arm."

When Casey was little his birth mother walked out, and he was taken care of by his father and a series of sitters. The father remarried when Casey was three, and the little boy was happy. Not long afterward a baby was born into the family, and things soon changed. Casey did not want to share his new mom with another person. It was difficult for Jill, too. Her life had never been a bed of roses, and she did not know how to cope with a clinging, crying three-year-old. Not only that, he took time with his father that was rightfully hers and her baby's. She told herself she wasn't jealous of a three-year-old, but she certainly was sick and tired of him.

Jill's solution for Casey's tantrums was to lock him in a closet. One afternoon Jill was doing laundry in the basement when she heard a terrible noise, then a scream. She ran upstairs. Somehow Casey had gotten out of the closet, taken the baby from its crib, and climbed to the top cupboard shelf, where he had stuffed the baby and closed the cupboard door. Getting down, Casey had fallen. For a moment Jill was furious, but when she saw the fear and pain on ·Casey's face she knew he was hurt. Casey had fractured his arm in the fall, and Jill knew she would have to take him to the emergency room. Running to get the baby, she found an empty crib! When Casey pointed to the cupboard shelf where he had put the baby, all the bratty things Casey did began to replay in her mind. She was so angry she was afraid to touch him for fear she would harm him. At the hospital, Casey's arm was put in a cast, and he was soothed and comforted. Jill was questioned about the injury, and the story came out of Casey's behavior toward the baby, Jill's solution of putting him in a closet, and Casey's retaliation. Social Services was called in. It was established that Casey had broken his arm in the fall; however, Social Services insisted that the family have counseling. The stepmother, recalling her rage and jealousy toward Casey, agreed. Talks with a psychologist went on for over a year, to good effect. Casey appears to be an alert, healthy, and good-natured teenager.

Casey's story has a good ending because his parents were willing to get counseling. Sadly, that did not happen in "Foolish Willie's" family:

> In the family drinking well
> Willie pushed his sister Nell.
> She's there yet, because it kilt her—
> Now we have to buy a filter.
>
> —*Anonymous*

THE INFLUENCE OF TELEVISION

During a half-hour TV program viewers are bombarded with four separate thirty-second commercials. These plugs go on at ten-minute intervals. Often the advertisements are subliminal, meaning that our brain gets the message without our consciously thinking about it. When we go to the mall, the supermarket, or a fast-food restaurant, we often know about a product because we have seen or heard about it on TV.

Everything from A to Z is advertised, hawked, pitched, and promoted on television. Teenage boys and girls the world over associate Michael Jordan with Nike. Sports figures like Larry Bird, Desmond Howard, Kareem Abdul-Jabbar, and Martina Navratilova, to name a few, endorse expensive sportswear. It's easy for young people to tell themselves they've got to have what the big-time athletes promote. Not only that, they *need* these things. Big-time sports figures influence our thinking, our goals, and certainly our wishes and wants. When a friend or someone we admire has something special, it's natural to want the same thing or something similar. Advertisers trade on this. Daily they assault us through million-dollar commercials and campaigns to entice us to buy their products. Sometimes when that is not possible, we are jabbed with the mean green finger of envy. That is more natural than not, more usual than unusual. It is how we handle our feelings that makes the difference.

It is not uncommon to hear of a theft resulting in murder when the victim refuses to give up a watch or jacket. Recently in Denver, a young boy was shot and his shoes were stolen. The only reason the perpetrator gave for his crime; "I wanted the Reboks, man. He had them and I didn't." Of course, that is an ugly example of envy mixed with a warped set of values. More often than not when we envy something and finally get it, an amazing thing happens: All the longing, envy, and jealousy were not worth the energy.

Television also gives the illusion that it can solve our romantic problems: Purchase the right brand of coffee. Show us how to be joyful: Buy a pizza. Find happiness: Apply for a loan to get a better car and a bigger house. Many people take these commercials seriously. "Balmy Willie" was one of them:

Willie with his eyes aglaze
Watched the TV many days.
"Buy me this and get me that,"
He yelled and snarled from where he sat.
　　　　　　　　　　　　—Beth Wilkinson

Frequently commercials are simple announcements about a product, but more often they tell a tale. A sixty-second commercial is much like any story of fiction, fable, or fantasy. It has a beginning, a middle, and an ending.

Try Magic Baby Powder

A new spot is currently being shown advertising a product for infants. It is wonderfully written and acted. The mother, baby, and small boy in the piece are three of the most beautiful people in the world. They are clean and shiny. The apartment, furniture, floor, and clothing are all so clean and shiny that you can almost smell the newness. The camera zooms in on a beautiful infant. Mom touches the infant lovingly. Infant gurgles. Mom looks toward the doorway. Small brother stands there looking sad, lonely, hurt—jealous. Small brother needs and wants some of the attention that beautiful infant is getting. Mom motions for small brother to help powder baby. Baby gurgles. Mom smiles. Brother smiles. All is well.

In real life it probably is not well at all. For all we know, small brother may be sticking beans up the nose of beautiful infant. Also, there's not a house with two small children on this planet that is so clean. But of course, the commercial is great. Thinking seriously, one realizes how responsible the media are for our emotions. Commercials insist that it is important to have anything we want.

What is really important is to have the insight to recognize a hard sell. Many people do, among them the father of "Wacky Willie":

> Willie's pa with thoughts so bright
> Said, "Willie, dear, that just ain't right."
> He barked right into Willie's ear,
> "You can't believe all that you hear."
> —*Beth Wilkinson*

Insight

The human being is born with five senses: the ability to feel, hear, touch, smell, and taste. There is another, sixth sense: insight. Insight is understanding and being aware of what is important when dealing with a problem. Insight also means the power of seeing into a situation. It is the perception or understanding of how others feel. A dictionary definition of insight is: an instance of apprehending the true nature of a thing, especially through intuitive understanding. Synonyms of insight are discernment, perception, and acumen.

When asked to complete the sentence: "I feel _____ when I am jealous," teenage boys and girls used the words *ugly, gross, sick, sad, hateful,* and *abused*. When asked to complete the sentence: "I feel _____ when I deliberately make someone jealous," boys and girls used the words: *mean, tired, mad,* and *abusive*. These teenagers readily agreed that a person needs insight to learn to cope with jealousy. Certainly these young people are gifted with this sixth sense. It is important that we have insight to recognize a hard sell. We need to develop this sixth sense so that we can take control of our emotions and not ultimately self-destruct.

Certainly insight was not one of Little Willie's better traits:

> Willie saw some dynamite,
> Couldn't understand it quite.
> Curiosity seldom pays:
> It rained Willie seven days.
>
> —*Anonymous*

Rule No. 4. Develop Insight.

CHAPTER 5

The Winterset Home for Boys and Girls

Winterset is a residential treatment facility for boys and girls ages thirteen to eighteen. These young people fall into the category of having serious emotional disturbance, also known as SED. The home is for children who are trying to get an education and learn coping skills in dealing with life. It is supported in a variety of ways: corporate and private donations and federal and state assistance. The school buildings, five in all, are modern, designed for comfortable living, and devoid of institutional features. Four supervisors and six houseparents live at Winterset; fifteen teachers commute from a nearby city.

The boys and girls at Winterset seem like the teenagers you would find at any public high school. That is far from the truth. These kids come from families with histories of physical, mental, and sexual abuse. They have had to live with the abandonment or indifference of absentee or exploitative parents. For them, seeing and committing serious acts of aggression have been commonplace. The problems that result are lack of confidence and concentration and a serious deficiency in judgment and motivation. Sudden anger, crushing bitterness, and overpowering jealousy arise. When a person has been neglected and unloved, relating to the most ordinary situations can be difficult. Getting through a day with acceptable behavior is often an unattainable goal. Education becomes a low priority when a person has been pulled, jerked, and yanked about for most of his or her life. Overwhelmed by family problems, these boys and girls respond by running away, attempting suicide, withdrawing, acting out sexually, and abusing drugs and alcohol.

Given a questionnaire and told they did not have to answer anything they didn't feel comfortable about, the boys and girls at Winterset were amazingly candid. To the question, "What is the *worst* thing you have ever done?" answers included: stole a car, told my mom I hated her, acted out of control, poisoned my sister's cat, made another person feel like garbage, beat up my brother, committed the crime of stealing, got in trouble with the law, stole from my parents, busted up some windows because my boyfriend was dancing with someone else, got drunk, and almost killed someone. To the question, "What is the *best* thing you've ever done?" some answers were: started running barrels for a rodeo, camping, and a pack trip.

It is interesting that the answers were fewer for the second question. Lee, age fifteen, answered the second question: "I saved a duck that swallowed a fishhook and was under water. I pulled him out."

Xavier

"Everyone in the world has been jealous at one time or another. When I got jealous it was over the most terrible thing in the world: money. I was so jealous that all my friends had more money than I did. I was always being a jerk about everything. It didn't take long before I had no friends left, but who needs friends anyway! I was looking high and low for cash. It didn't matter whether it was legal or not. So now I had two problems: jealousy and greed. Because of my jealousy I was sent to jail, and then to a boys' home. I now live at Winterset at the age of seventeen. The biggest reason I am here is because I was jealous and greedy. Jealousy sucks. I look back and can't believe how stupid I was. My favorite author, S.E. Hinton, once said, 'That was then, this is now!' These few words are what keep me from making the same mistakes over and over. *I try to remember: That was then, this is now.*"

The goals of the staff at Winterset include creation of a consistent family-living environment and a structured school, recreation, and work schedule. Group therapy, individual counseling, and psychiatric services are also part of the program. Lynn, age fifteen, a resident for two years, sums up her life at Winterset. "I am learning to act in an responsible manner," she says with pride and dignity.

Visitors are welcome at Winterset, and it is a pleasure to observe the different levels of reading and English classes. Because they are pleased to have a guest in their midst, the young people are easy to work with. They are friendly and eager to exchange ideas about their schoolwork. Their attitude is impressive, for their visitor is someone who, they fantasize, could be a long-lost maiden aunt or a forgotten grandmother. "You have sparky eyes like my mom had," Eli says, out of the hearing of his fellow students. They are silent when read to. The book of poetry, its cover threadbare, holds magic. The listeners have transported themselves into the Victorian past of Robert Frost's "Stopping by Woods on a Snowy Evening:"

> He gives his harness bells a shake
> To ask if there is some mistake.
> The only other sound's the sweep
> Of easy wind and downy flake.

Their complete attention is a delight to the reader's soul. From their intent looks, the children have for a short time escaped the sadness of their fractured worlds.

When asked to name a hero, they became serious, but some of the boys and girls showed some humor, too. Their list included: Mother Cabrini, Kermit the Frog, Michael Jordan, Kiss, and What's a hero? The question, "What are you going to be when you grow up?" brought realistic as well as unrealistic answers: a nurse, an engineer, a veterinarian, a secretary, an astronaut, a millionaire, and a genius.

A discussion of memories evoked reminiscences of early childhood. "I remember my dog, Toby," Eli said. "I remember a birthday party where I had a beautiful cake and balloons," Zoe told us. However, most early memories involved being frightened, yelled at, and physically injured. Lynn said, "My dad was always beating on my mom. Right in front of me he would hit Mom, smash her face. Sometimes he would knock her cold. It was not a nice time."

When things go right these students appear exhilarated, but when things go wrong they take a sudden plunge into the depths of despair. For most of the residents, behavior at Winterset is much like a roller coaster ride. Perhaps with all the hurts these young people have experienced, it is natural to be excessive in emotions they experience. "We have lots of displays of jealousy here," the supervisor explains. "With a student body of fourteen girls and twice as many boys, it's unavoidable. They are jealous when a girl pays special attention to a boy that everyone likes or when a popular boy is attentive to several of the girls. Sometimes the behavior gets out of control and ends in a fistfight or hair-pulling. On the other hand, we have some great success stories. We strive not only to educate our boys and girls but to instill the importance of accountability. When students start learning to cope with problems, they begin making plans for their future. That is a great triumph for everyone at Winterset."

Writing about Feelings

Zoe, a pretty and vibrant young woman, has lived at Winterset for almost two years. When Miss Laurie assigned her the topic of jealousy to write about, she took it seriously. "I am familiar with this feeling," she said with a shrug. The finished essay, seven short sentences, is outstanding. It shows the insight of a person far more mature than her thirteen years.

> "Jealousy is a horrible feeling. Jealousy hurts your 'feelers'. Jealousy hurts a friendship. Jealousy hurts family relations. Jealousy hurts the mind. Jealousy causes depression. Jealousy causes the silent treatment to begin. Jealousy is a negative feeling."

The following stories about jealousy were written by boys and girls ages thirteen to fifteen. They are students in a self-contained classroom at Winterset. Classes are conducted by two teachers, Ms. Torres and Miss Laurie, and one male attendant whom everyone calls Bear.

Alexandra

"One evening I was walking down the street and saw my best friend, Rita. She came over and said, 'I'm sorry, I can't go to the movies with you this weekend, I'm going with someone else.' I just walked away hurt, thinking about how she had spoken to me: 'I'm sorry,' she says. I get tired of hearing people tell me they're sorry. I kept walking, but I heard her say, 'She's a poor sport.' I walked faster and faster and started to cry. I started to run. I didn't want anyone to see me. I was so jealous that she had another friend. I depend on Rita. We go everywhere together and are always partners in gym or when we ride the bus to town. I was mad. I felt miserable. I ran to my room, slammed the door, and started blasting Ozzy Osbourne. A counselor came in and asked what was wrong. I explained about how Rita had found someone that she liked better than me. The counselor said I needed to work at having more than one friend. I told her it was not possible because I'm so ugly and fat. I cried myself asleep. The next morning I saw Rita and she said, 'Alex, I'm so sorry. I didn't mean to hurt you.' I felt better, but I can't forget how it was when I thought I had lost the only person in this world I depend on to be there for me. I felt like a wrung-out dishrag. I apologized to my counselor. I don't like feeling jealous. It's too crazy."

Seth

"When I was in regular school there was a boy in my class that would beat me out the door every day at lunch time. He was also the first person to finish with his work. The teacher would write stuff on his papers like 'Bravo' and 'Good Show'. Sometimes she would put a fancy Chiquita banana sticker on his paper. I always wished I had one. I was jealous of him because he got all the breaks and all the glory. This guy always put his head down on his desk and took a nap. One day just before lunch when he was sleeping I tied his shoelaces to the leg of his desk. The teacher didn't even see me. When the lunch bell sounded the kid woke up and ran for the door, only he fell flat on his face. I suppose it was a pretty rotten thing to do. I'm not sorry I did it because I couldn't help being jealous."

Lynn

"I get jealous of the attention my sister gets. When I was home I asked my parents for a bird, a mouse, and a rabbit. I was hoping for two out of three. My parents said no way. My sister asked for a bird, a mouse, a rabbit, and a hamster—a regular zoo! They let her have the hamster. That's more than I got. Now that I'm away from home my sister gets all my mom's attention and yes, I am jealous of my sister."

Eli

"I am jealous when I see a mother, a dad, and their kids going into McDonald's, Wendy's, or Burger

King. I get mad. Sometimes I cry. I wish I had a family that had turkey for Thanksgiving. We would sit at a big table. They would laugh and not be drunk. They would not holler and yell. When I am grown-up I will get my kids an Atari and roller-blades. I will not put them down. They will not be jealous."

Lorraine

"My youth worker, Mrs. West, is going to have a baby in February. I'm ashamed to tell this, but I'm jealous of her baby. It's true and it's dumb and I can't help it. I hate to admit that I'm jealous of someone that isn't even born. This baby is going to come into the world to a family that's loving, caring, and supportive of everything it does. This baby is going to have an easier life than I did because it will have people around it to teach it lessons. Here I am, almost sixteen, and I'm only now learning manners that everyone else knows about. Mrs. West's baby will know how to get along, how to control anger, and how to trust because her parents are going to tell her what's right. Girl or boy, that baby will be ahead of what I am by the time it's in the first grade. I wish I had parents like Mr. and Mrs. West."

THE OTHER SIDE OF THE COIN

Cameron and Babs Elsworth are brother and sister. The house where they live is situated on twenty acres and has eight rooms, four baths, and a three-car garage. The slate roof, cathedral windows, and a tree-lined driveway leading up to the big front doors are handsome and impressive.

The distance from the Winterset Home to the Elsworths' small estate is only a few miles. However, the difference in life-styles is comparable to the distance from Minnesota to the moon.

Cameron

"I have a friend, Rodney, and he can do anything he wants to do. For example, if he gets grounded and can't go skiing, it means his parents won't take him. He can still go with the guys. When I'm grounded, I'm grounded. No television, allowance, movies, or going to McDonald's. Nothing. I stay in my room. Rodney has more freedom than I have, and I'm jealous of that. Another thing, if I want to rent a couple of movies my dad says one movie is enough. Rodney asks to rent three movies and his mom says he can get two. He's a major mouth and can convince them he needs to get three. It works. All his mom says is for him not to whine. I tried that with my dad. He said to forget it, one movie was enough. It seems to me that Rodney's parents don't tell him what to do. He tells them. Rodney has power I don't have."

Babs

"I feel jealous when someone else receives an award or position that I want. I'm an honor-roll student. That is expected of me. I like being on the volleyball team and on committees, too. I never compete for friends, but I do compete to get elected to an office in Student Council, Drama Club, and German Club. I like belonging to a lot of organizations. I like sports, too. One of my friends was all-conference in volleyball. I took her to lunch to celebrate, but I was jealous. The things I get jealous of read like a shopping list, only not as nice. 1. I am jealous of Susan because she is an awesome volleyball player. 2. I am jealous of Augusta and Heidi because they have beautiful voices and sing the leads in choir; I can't sing to save my life. 3. I am jealous of Amy because she is so outgoing and personable. She can talk to guys very easily. 4. I am jealous of Daphne because her family is well off; rich, rich, rich. She is going to go to a private school in New Jersey; I wish I could go there or to a school like it. 5. I am jealous of Joanne because we were so close in volleyball, then she went on into varsity. I sat on the bench most of the time while she was the most important member on her team. 6. I am jealous of other people's personalities—people who are outgoing, high-spirited, funny, and are able to talk to others easily. 7. I am jealous of people who have nice bodies, are good-looking and liked by all the guys.

"It seems stupid for me to feel this way. I take so many things for granted, like having a family that is together, when a lot of my friends' parents are divorced. I feel guilty when I am envious of my friends. I probably waste time being jealous when I could put thoughts and efforts toward something more productive."

Cameron

"The most popular kid at Junior High is Ace Crocker. All the girls say he is aces, meaning he's a stud or the best. He's an athlete, and everyone knows who he is. He wears perfectly torn jeans, which Mom refuses to let me wear, and he doesn't know anyone who isn't popular. For Ace they don't exist. The kids I eat lunch with make fun of his name. We always make jokes, the gist of which is not printable. Of course we're all jealous. Who wouldn't want to be Ace Crocker?"

Babs

"This makes me jealous: people who have strong relationships with their brothers or sisters. All siblings fight, but we never get along. I wish Cameron would just be my friend. I wish he would acknowledge me as a person. We could do things like go to the mall or to a movie. Once we went to a movie and he didn't even sit by me. That really hurt. He wouldn't go Christmas shopping with me this year, and then he went with Rodney that same day."

Cameron

"Rodney does not show my parents respect, and it bugs me. Mom and Dad seem to handle it really good, like they'll say, 'Rodney, you don't need to talk like that when you're here.' They're awful nice. I guess they know I hang out with Rod because he's the only kid my age that lives in this neighborhood. We take the school bus together, and it's a lot easier going with Rodney because everyone else lives across town. Besides, we're both into science and building structures with Legos. Also, he's a real comedian and he knows a lot of magic tricks that I haven't been able to figure out. We trade books a lot, because we're really into C.S. Lewis and Tolkien and Rod has a lot of paperbacks that I don't have. I don't think it's right for me to be jealous of him. My sister says I'll learn how to manage my feelings better as I grow up. That's what she says, "manage." My sister talks funny but she's okay."

DIFFERENCES

The living conditions, attitudes, and desires of the children at Winterset and the Elsworths are miles apart. The Wintersets yearn for the love of parents or a parent. They fantasize about a future where there is stability and kindness. On the other hand Cameron and Babs Elsworth have experienced the nurturing and love of a family since the day of their birth. They do not foresee blips on their screens of life, whereas the kids at Winterset, bruised by hurt all of their young years, have limited expectations. They have not been taught coping skills and have stronger displays of emotion. The spectrum of what makes the Winterset kids angry and jealous is different. Eli longs for family ties. He becomes jealous when he sees young people going to a fast-food place with their parents. To be envious of that kind of situation would never enter Cameron's head. He and his family frequent any restaurant they choose. They have been to Disneyland, Disney World, and the Epcot Center. Although Cameron does not participate in sports, he is a spectator and has been to the Copper Bowl in Tucson and the Holiday Bowl in San Diego. Going to places that he takes for granted would boggle the minds of Lee, Xavier, Zoe, Seth, Lynn, and Lorraine. In their world, going to Narnia or the Bermuda Triangle is just as likely. For them, having a family vacation or even a family picnic is what dreams are made of.

Cameron's jealousy lies in the fact that his best friend, Rodney, gets by when he exhibits outrageous behavior to his parents. Cameron admits that Rod is often a jerk. He feels jealous that Rod has the dubious power of manipulating his parents and getting away with it.

There is also a difference in the jealousy felt by Alexandra and by Babs. Alex has one friend she depends on. When Rita said she was going to a movie with someone else, Alexandra showed jealous by overreacting: She slammed drawers and played loud music. She calls herself derogatory names like fat and ugly, which are not true. Babs, who has many friends, feels jealous when someone outdoes her in academics or sports. She does well at controlling her feelings but is plagued by guilt because she feels jealous.

Feelings of jealousy are equally serious in the minds of Eli, Alexandra, Cameron, and Babs. Eli is jealous because he feels shortchanged in family relations. Alex feels cheated in the friends department. Cameron and Babs feel jealous when they think their abilities don't match their ambitions. However, all four agree on how they would like to handle these emotions.

Eli

"I talk a lot to the counselor, Mr. Walseth. He's a good person. He has several horses and says he's liked horses since he was my age. Sometimes he takes me horseback riding. He says that the best thing to do when I feel mad or jealous is to remove myself from the scene. I try to do that. I talk things out with Mr. Walseth."

Alexandra

"I am learning to control my anger and jealousy. When someone snubs me I pretend not to notice. I always tell my friend Rita, and we talk about it. That's the best way for me."

Cameron

"Life for me on a scale of ten is an eight or a nine. I know I'm a lucky guy. When I feel jealous I try not to hold it inside. I try to make a joke about it or shrug it off."

Babs

"I try not to worry about my jealousy. Even when I know it's there, I try not to dwell on it. Sometimes I talk it over with Mom."

Rule No. 5. Talk about Feelings.

CHAPTER 6

Perceptions

Sticks and stones
May break my bones
But names will never hurt me.

There are two meanings here. Name-calling is one. The other refers to personal names. Let's face it, some monikers are harder to live with than others. In America, boys' names tend to be traditional. When selecting a name for a daughter, parents seem to prefer something more fashionable. It is not unusual for both boys and girls from nine into the teen years to change their names. Most often a nickname is a boy's choice, whereas girls seem more concerned about trendy names.

In our country, people normally have three names; a first, a middle, and a family name. Adults often use the initial of their middle name. This distinguishes them from other people with the same first and family names. People who do not have a middle name write their name on legal documents as John NMI Jones or Rose NMI Smith, NMI meaning No Middle Initial.

People are hurt and made jealous about the most surprising, and unimportant, things. Not having a middle name or a nickname is one of them. Middle names and nicknames are usually chosen with care. They are important signs of affection. Seventeen-year-old Jacob feels he has been cheated because he was never given a nickname. He has an interesting story and a legitimate complaint.

Jacob

Jacob and Joshua were twins. Joshua died at the age of fifteen in a rock-climbing accident. The family always called him Josh. Jacob feels his family loved the dead twin more because they gave him a nickname. "When I asked Dad why he didn't call me Jake, he said, 'Because that's what your grandfather is called.' I wanted to ask what that had to do with anything, but I didn't."

Clearly, Jacob needs to get his feelings out in the open and discuss what he sees as hurtful and unfair. His problem is serious, and he may even need help in resolving it. Others feel the same way. Pearl and Dorothy both say they are jealous of people who have middle names.

Pearl

Pearl says she was named after a great-aunt. "They always say she was a gem. I guess they never stopped to think that a pearl may be a gem but it started out as sand that got trapped in an oyster. Great. I have such a plain name, the least my parents could have done was give me a middle name with sex appeal; something like Marietta, or Sasha, or Crystal. They didn't even give me a nickname. When I finish school and get a job, I may go to court and get a middle name. I may even get a new first name."

Changing a name or adopting a new name is neither expensive nor difficult. Going through a court formality is often not necessary. The best way to change or add a name is to drop the old and add the new. Use the chosen one whenever and wherever possible. As long as you do not intend to break the law, it is legal to call yourself whatever you like.

Dorothy

"Almost the first question I ask anyone is, 'What's your middle name?' My sister says I'm obsessed. Sure, she can say that. Her name is Margaret Rose. Mom says my grandmother named her after the king of England's youngest daughter. The king's oldest daughter is now Queen Elizabeth II. Once I looked up her name, and it's Elizabeth Alexandra Mary. She has *two* middle names and dozens of fancy titles. Maybe that comes with a queendom. Since one of my grandmas named my sister, my other grandmother got to name me. She named me after Dorothy in 'The Wizard of Oz,' her favorite movie when she was a kid. I told Mom the least the family could do is to call me Dot or Dottie. But no, I'm not even allowed a nickname. Last year I hung out with Jack Kelly, and I told him I had two middle names. I said my name was Dorothy Alexandra Mary Albright, almost like the queen of England's. I wonder if that's why he quit calling me. Of course. That and because he started going with another senior named Candy. Her middle name is probably Cane, or Case. Maybe it's Bar. Candy is okay, and I'm only a little jealous of her. Jack's a hunk. All the girls like him."

Jack smiled when asked about Candy, but he only shrugged about Dorothy's middle-name dilemma. However, he did have a contribution, not only about second names but about jealousy too.

Jack

"All I know about middle names is that most people have them. I was named after John Fitzgerald Kennedy. In History 502 we've studied most of our Presidents like Franklin Delano Roosevelt and Richard Milhouse Nixon. Roosevelt and Nixon signed their names using middle initials. With names like Delano and Milhouse it was a good move. I learned in a trivia game that Harry Truman didn't have a middle name, only an S for a middle initial. Maybe it stood for shortchanged, as in shortchanged of a middle name."

ADVICE FROM A TEENAGER

Jack has bigger worries than middle names. He has a nephew he thinks is terrific, but "pretty spoiled." Patrick is three and a half, and before his baby sister was born he could have been described as the perfect child. His parents had Patrick tested by a psychologist and are proud of the fact that he has a high I.Q. He is handsome, with long black eyelashes and curling red hair. He can read, draw pictures of recognizable horses, imitate Elvis, and recite any nursery rhyme he ever heard. He has two sets of adoring grandparents, doting aunts and uncles, idolizing great-aunts and uncles, and a loving great-grandmother.

When expecting their second child, Patrick's parents

did everything possible to make sure their son would accept the new baby. They read the latest child-care books and magazines and went to a series of lectures. When a daughter was born everyone was overjoyed. At one month Moira has long dark eyelashes, mounds of red hair, and dimples. She is beautiful. "My lovely Irish colleen," her grandfather Kelly calls her. Patrick is in a frenzy. In spite of all the assurance and love given him by the family, he is unreasonably jealous. When anyone picks up Moira, Patrick explodes. "Pick me up!" he yells. The family are at their wits' end. They are worried, and it shows on their tired faces. Everyone tries to help. Patrick is given gifts by his grandparents and taken for special lunches and trips to the zoo. His jealousy has not lessened. He is not learning to cope with his feelings.

Patrick's uncle Jack has observed and taken in the whole picture.

Jack Again

"I think Pat will eventually stop the Tasmanian devil act, but in the meantime it's hard to be around my brother's family. They're always telling Pat what to do and not do. He's *baaad*. He hits the dog, tries to choke the cat, and turns over his milk glass regularly. He does stuff like that to get attention. Patrick's like the kid in a rhyme I've heard him say: He found the bellows, and he blew/The pet canary right in two! That's another thing. People should be careful what they say around Pat. They should be careful what they teach him, too, because he takes things seriously.

"When my brother and his wife try to talk Pat out of his tantrums, it's like watching the Three Stooges. Everyone acts crazy like Larry, Moe, and Curly. My nephew is a good kid, but he can't stand for anyone to pay attention to the baby. He throws tantrums like you never heard. I have a feeling that what Pat is really learning, with all the attention everyone gives him, is how to manipulate people.

"I always try to be honest with my brother. When he asked if I thought there was a problem, I said "Soitanly." Then I got serious and gave him my advice. I told him that Patrick is given too many material things. When he's rotten, people bribe him with toys and take him places. That doesn't make sense to me. My brother said he thinks Patrick will grow out of his tantrums. I told him, 'In your dreams'."

Tantrums

What Jack and his brother probably don't know is that most children stop having tantrums around the age of four. Maybe this is because they interact more with other children. Enter peer pressure. A child is less likely to act badly around friends. What Jack does recognize is that Patrick is learning to manipulate others. Even at eighteen, Jack knows that his family indulges Pat too much. Jack probably knows, too, that it would be more effective to reward Patrick for good behavior than bad behavior.

A Camp-Out

On a fishing trip, a group of happy teenage campers were asked, "What makes you jealous?" Around a flickering fire and stuffed with fried fish and potatoes, the young people answered in round-robin fashion, like a continuing tack-on ghost story.

"Can you believe I felt jealous at my big sister's wedding shower. For a present I gave her a fire-engine red whistling tea kettle. Wouldn't you know, someone gave her an electric one? When Sissy saw it her eyes got big, and I knew she was impressed. Someone outdid me. I had this mean feeling. Mean and green."

"The fish were great, but I only caught two of the small ones. I wish I'd caught that two-pound brown trout. Todd caught it, but I would feel better if it had been me. Sorry, Todd."

"I'm not jealous of anything, but my cat gets upset when the neighbor's cat, Mr. Kitty, comes to our window. I pay attention to him because he's a stitch; he rolls over, chases his tail, and shakes his head like he's telling me the Rangers beat the Bills. My cat smacks at the window and yowls. I'm sure if I let Mr. Kitty in the house my cat would go berserk."

"I go berserk when I see kids strut their stuff in the Rose Parade. I know I play the clarinet as well as any of those kids. When you're in a hot marching band you get to go places, and the Rose Parade is one of them."

"I'd be jealous if a friend won a million-dollar sweep-stakes or a lottery. I wonder what it would be like? You could buy the world. Sometimes Ed McMahon is in my fantasy handing me a check for a cool million bucks."

Obviously everyone on the camp-out was in a great mood. It was easy to laugh and make fun of their jealousy, because none of it was serious. Sad but true, not all jealousy is so laid back. For many people with a jealous nature, competition is important and winning is a must.

HOW OTHERS HANDLE IT

Lu Chen, Eugene Calhoun, Spike Renfro, and a seventeen-year-old with the wonderful name of Grace Whitefeather all go to the same high school. They are freshman, sophomore, junior, and senior, respectively. All four are serious about their jealousy and recognize what causes it. They also do not find solutions too difficult.

Lu Chen came from Qing Dao, China, two years ago. His English was minimal, but he now speaks well. Because of government policy, Chen came to the United States a year after his parents, Cia Ping and Lu Pong. In America Ping and Pong have lots of fun with their names, and Chen thinks it's pretty funny, too. He deserves a laugh these days. Life has not been easy for him and his family. Many times at ages eleven and twelve Chen traveled 500 miles from his home to the Embassy in Beijing to get a passport to cross the ocean and join his mother and father. He was refused six times. On his seventh trip he was given permission. Chen's parents are university students and take education seriously. So does Chen.

Lu Chen

"Last year I knew a boy who was very nice. This year we are in class together. We are both in honors English and honors math. He is not so nice this year. He does mean things like putting bad-word stickers on other people's backs. I always get the top grade in the class because I work hard and don't watch television. When my grades are the best, he calls me dumb. Sometimes I answer back by saying, 'You are dumber.' He always asks me questions in math. When I got my report card he wanted to see my grades, and his face became unpleasant. He said, 'I just didn't try hard enough.' That was only an excuse. I believe he did his best but just doesn't want to admit it. He is jealous. It is better to ignore him."

Eugene Calhoun

"Last year I had a growth spurt. I'm fifteen and over six feet tall. I think people have different expectations of a person who is tall, even if he's skinny. I can't be any different than I am. I've always been quiet, because that's the way I've always felt—quiet. I don't have many friends, and everyone else does. I feel jealous about that. I'm happier not being in junior high. There's more freedom in high school. We have an hour for lunch as opposed to a half hour in junior high. When I'm in lunch line, friends give cuts. I've been standing in line forever and someone gives a friend cuts. I get angry about that, but I get jealous, too.

"Another thing, some people have money and I don't. They can buy anything they want without their parents' say-so. Not me. I live with my mom, and her income is not great. Money is hard to get. No one will hire me until I'm sixteen. I do get odd jobs, but I don't earn enough to buy much. My granddad hires me for a lawn job, but that's only in the summer. I can't lie about my age because everyone wants identification. I can't lie anyhow. Who wants to be a liar? Besides, the person who hired me could get into trouble and I would get fired.

"I'm doing okay, better than when I was in eighth

grade. At least, I think so. I try to talk and compliment others. I do my best. If people like me it's okay, but if they don't that's their choice, too. Sometimes I think about how great it would be to be like Michael Jordan—slam balls, be respected, have a lot of money, meet fans, and know girls. Mom says time takes care of a lot of feelings. Well, I'm waiting, I'm waiting."

Grace Whitefeather

"This year I signed up for a marketing class at school. Students in the program have release time for on-the-job training in an office, a business, or a shop of some kind. The class slogan is 'Invest in Your Future'. Students earn credit as well as pay. This works for me. The object is to learn how to get a job and keep it. My teacher calls it competing in the workplace, only he usually says the real world. Because my grades had improved over my sophomore year, I was given a fantastic assignment, which is actually called a training station. For ten hours a week, two hours a day, I work as an intern in the education department at the state university. I take the school bus to the high school, and the U is within walking distance from there. The woman I work for is a Ph.D. candidate, which means she is working for an advanced degree. Ms. Lacy is very nice and considerate. My job involves using a computer, filing, and answering the telephone. I'm also learning to make educational videos. It's hard and complicated, but it's exciting work. I'm learning about what goes on in an office, too, and it's not all good. Somewhere I heard about professional jealousy, but it never made sense to me. I always thought a person went to work, did the job, then went home or wherever. Simple, right? Wrong. It is not simple to have a job. It is important to learn people skills, which means getting along with others.

"Ms. Lacy gets along because she always plays it cool when the department head, Dr. Farmer, gets difficult. He is a very jealous person. I think he is also incompetent, because lots of times he has to ask *me* how to connect, find, or sort out stuff. He is also unprofessional. He takes long lunch hours and coffee breaks and plays golf when the weather is good. Naturally it falls on everyone else to do his work and theirs, too. It seems he's jealous because people prefer to work with Ms. Lacy or other staff members on special assignments. Dr. Farmer was furious when she asked for time off to attend an out-of-state workshop. It was a real opportunity for her to learn new techniques in videotaping. There's not much of a budget at the department, so Ms. Lacy offered to pay her own expenses. Finally she convinced him. The workshop included well-known speakers and hands-on experience, and Ms. Lacy told me it had been a definite plus.

"When she was asked to give a presentation on what she had learned about developing educational video games, she gave me an assignment. I worked my buns off getting it done right. I got permission from my high school principal to attend the presentation, and the turnout was great. Ms. Lacy received a lot of compliments and was asked to give another lecture at a later date. I felt good about that. I knew my hard work had paid off. That's what Ms. Lacy said. The boss, the head honcho, Dr. Farmer never said a word. Not one word. No cheers, applause, not even a bravo. Zip. When I told Ms. Lacy I thought the boss was mean, she only smiled and told me to forget it. Trust me, it is depressing to be around a person with a jealous nature.

"I know now that jealousy is not only a selfish feeling but can be subtly expressed as harassment. I hope when I finish school and work in the real world I'll be able to cope with jealousy if my boss happens to have that kind of nature."

Spike Rutherford

"My girlfriend has this great bod. She has a tiny waist and looks fantastic in jeans, which is what she wears most of the time. When we go anyplace—to the mall, a concert, a basketball game—guys always turn around or give her a second look. It really burns me, yet I'm proud of her, too. I hate to admit it, but maybe I'm jealous."

Spike is probably aware that heads often turn in his direction, for he is a nice-looking boy and well liked by his peers. That very fact, no doubt, gives him the confidence to admit to an occasional pang of jealousy.

Rule No. 6. Learn to Cope, Cope, Cope.

CHAPTER ◇ 7

Talk Shows

People related by marriage, adoption, or blood are called family members, kin, relations, and sometimes, playfully, shirttail relatives. People in these categories are mothers, fathers, sons, daughters, sisters, half-sisters, brothers, half-brothers, aunts, uncles, grandmothers, grandfathers, cousins, nephews, and nieces. Relationships by marriage include brothers-in-law, sisters-in-law, fathers-in-law, and mothers-in-law, stepbrothers, stepsisters, stepfathers, stepmothers, stepsons, and stepdaughters. Family relationships include people in foster families, adopted families, and extended families. In the everyday world there are as many combinations of relatives as there are combinations of jealousies.

When a death or divorce has been followed by establishment of a new family, there may be more challenges in coping with jealousy. A household of "her kids, his kids, and our kids" is not unusual: Two adults with children have remarried, and a child or children have resulted from the union. Depending on how situations are handled, this can be either a difficult or a wonderful life-style for those involved. A more precarious state is when a family

82

or a newly formed family is dysfunctional; when alcohol or
drugs are used and abuse is part of the scenario.

Jealousy often arises when a man or woman remarries
and starts another family. The mother or father may
appear to bond more with the new family or seem closer
to the older children. Jealousy among stepbrothers and
stepsisters is common. Lewis Keyes put his stepbrother
on a pedestal but was wise enough to figure out that he
himself is every bit as special.

Lewis Keyes

"Ian and I met as toddlers, when our mothers took us
to the park to play. In school he was always one of
the smartest kids in class and always nice to everyone. I was proud to be his friend. Ian was big and
mature-looking for his age. When we were ten and
went to Saturday afternoon movies he always had to
show an ID because the cashier thought he should
pay for an adult ticket.

"Something else happened when we were ten: Our
parents got divorces and my mom married his dad.
It's a whole different story, but I guess it happens in
some families. It worked out okay, and we were both
old enough to know that life is not always fair. Ian
and I talked about it a lot. We had each other. We
were stepbrothers, and we were able to get away
from all the trouble our folks had.

"In junior high the girls were crazy about Ian,
because he was so smooth. He even started shaving.
In high school he was a good dancer, played the
piano, and was the state wrestling champion in his
weight division. We were always tight, but he was
the poppy-bod, which I call people who are con-

sidered popular bodies. I worshiped Ian and always knew he would make it big. When he turned thirteen he was invited to sing with a big orchestra in the El Paso city auditorium. He was fantastic, and the crowd went crazy. I remember that I felt good when his voice changed and he couldn't sing as well as he did when he was a couple of years younger.

"Anyway, one day it dawned on me that I'd grown taller than Ian, I played the piano enough to impress my girlfriend, and it was okay that I'd never be a wrestling champion or sing like a rock star because that wasn't my thing. It dawned on me too that my brother wasn't all that smooth, that actually he was full of crapola like all the rest of the guys. It was a great awakening. I hate to think I was jealous of Ian all those years, but I probably was. I'd built him up in my mind to be more than he was. Ian was a good guy and always will be. The only thing is, he was probably never a whole lot different than me."

Lewis was wise enough to realize that he deserved a pedestal as much as Ian.

PITCH, PUBLICITY, AND PRESENTATION

Probably the most common, and perhaps the most volatile, is the jealousy between mother and teenage daughter in vying for male attention—often the young girl's boyfriends. This type of discord is the perfect topic for television talk shows.

For a number of years the airwaves have been filled with talk shows. Many of these programs open doors to truth and touch upon the social ills of our society. If you have a bad situation, some of these programs are bound to address some of your questions. Discussing problems, trying to understand different viewpoints, and hearing expert counsel can be helpful and worthwhile. Hearing what others have to say can give a person another viewpoint.

Sometimes, however, talk show hosts urge their guests into making hurtful, thoughtless statements about their friends and families, and audiences weigh in with personal opinions and sometimes reckless advice. This is what usually happens when the topic of jealousy is discussed on any talk show in the country. Not long ago a program addressed the jealousy often felt between mothers and daughters.

The host introduces Storm and her daughter, Breezy, to the studio audience by saying, "My guest today says her mother is too sexy. The daughter doesn't like it. Breezy says her mom is so beautiful and sexy, it's sickening. She also says she resents the way her mom competes with her for guys when they go out together."

Storm is thirty-five years old, with long blonde hair, shoulder-length feather earrings, and heavy eye makeup. She is dressed in a short leather miniskirt and a low-cut satin blouse. She gestures a lot, and her bright red fingernails catch the light.

Breezy is sixteen. With hair styled in scrunch fashion, she wears similar earrings and eye makeup, baggies, and a Disneyland sweatshirt. Like her mother, she gestures a lot. Her fingernails are bitten to the quick.

"First of all," the host says, "let's talk about the problem. Breezy, tell us your side of the story."

"Well, look at Mom. Look at the way she dresses..."

The mother quickly interrupts and continues to do so throughout the program. "There's nothing wrong with the way I dress."

Breezy:	Yes, there is. It's sleazy. You don't look like a mom. Why can't you dress like other people?
Storm:	Like how?
Breezy:	You know, jeans, tennis shoes, a sweater. You look great in jeans, but every time we go somewhere you wear things that make you look like a . . . I don't want to say it.
Storm:	Go ahead and say it.
Breezy:	A slut. There, I've said it. You look like a slut!
Storm:	No way. You've got to be kidding, Breezy.
Host:	Today's mother of forty—and your mom is only thirty-five—is very young-looking. What do you want, a television mom?"
Breezy:	Yeah, I want a mom that looks good in jeans.
Host:	The baggy type?
Breezy:	My mom would never wear baggies. She wears Lycra leggings two sizes too small.
Host:	You won't wear baggies?
Storm:	Never. I like to show off what I have, and that's a 38 bust and a 26 waist. If I look good in something, why not wear it?
Host:	Okay. Okay. So you and your mom go to a club together, right? By the way, what kind of a club is this?"
Breezy:	It's a private club and very nice. We have dinner and there's a dance floor,

	and sometimes guys ask us to dance, only they always ask her first.
Host:	And you don't like that.
Breezy:	No. The last time we went a guy asked her to dance and they danced all night. I just sat by myself while they danced and rubbed up against each other. It was sickening. He only did it because of the way she was dressed.
Storm:	I think I looked good. The guy said I looked good.
Breezy:	You looked slutty.
Storm:	C'mon, I dress sexy and I happen to like a lot of satin and lace. I like leather, too. Why not?
Breezy:	Because you embarrass me with the skimpy see-through blouses, that's why. You should dress like a mother.
Storm:	Don't should on me, Baby.
(Audience laughs)	
Breezy:	It was sickening. He was too young for her. I even dated him a few times. He's closer to my age.
Storm:	I have a personality, too.
Breezy:	The guy was not interested in your personality, and you know it.
Host:	Is he still in school?
Breezy:	I think he graduated from high school last year. He's still too young for her.
Host:	I'm sure members of this audience have some ideas on this problem of being jealous of a sexy mom.
1st Audience Member:	I don't really think this mother and daughter should be going on dates

	together. It's ridiculous.
Storm:	Excuse me. Excuse me. If your daughter asked you to go with her and, you know, have a little fun . . . I mean, they're her friends and my friends.
1st Audience Member:	I dress sexy when I go out with my husband. There's a place and time.
Breezy:	Yeah.
Storm:	Why wouldn't you go out with your daughter?
1st Audience Member:	I wouldn't want to take away from my daughter. Even if I could. She's got her time. I had mine.
Storm:	Well, you need time together, don't you?
1st Audience Member:	I want her to respect me as her mother.
Storm:	So you're married?
1st Audience Member:	Yes, I am.
Storm:	Well, I'm not, and my daughter and I have a good relationship. We like going out together.
Host:	But there's a problem when you do go out, isn't there?
Breezy:	Yes. She dresses sleazy. She hits on my boyfriends and I'm tired of it. I really love my mom. I think she's beautiful, but she doesn't act like a mother. She tries to be my girlfriend. She tells me stuff I don't want to know.
Host:	Like what?

Breezy: Personal stuff about her and guys.
               What I really resent, what really bugs
               me is how she dresses and how she
               walks. She carries herself like, "Look
               at me. Look at what I've got."

Storm: Well, if you got it, flaunt it, is what
               I say.

(Applause.)

2nd Audience   Your mother is really beautiful.
   Member:

3rd Audience   I want to say that your mom is
   Member: gorgeous. You know what I think?
               Okay, I'll say it. You're jealous
               because you're not that attractive. If
               my—.

Breezy: Me? You think I'm jealous? Look at
               her. She's hanging out of her blouse,
               for gosh sakes. You think I'm jealous
               of that?

3rd Audience   Excuse me. If my mother wanted to
   Member: hang out with me, she could, any day.

(Laughter.)

Breezy: What does your mother look like?

3rd Audience   She's nice-looking. Better looking
   Member: than I am.

Breezy: Sure, and she wears an apron when
               she cooks, right? I'd like that, but
               that's not my mother. We eat at fast-
               food places, the club, or snooty
               restaurants most of the time. I can't
               remember the last time I had a home-
               cooked meal. The way my mom looks
               and acts isn't fair.

4th Audience   Couldn't you cook a meal? You cer-

Member:	tainly don't look helpless. You look like a very healthy girl.
Breezy:	For Thanksgiving Mom got us chicken boxes at Kentucky Fried. Whoopee!
5th Audience Member:	We seem to be getting away from the subject. My question is directed to Storm. When you go out with your daughter, why don't you dress more discreetly?
Storm:	Why should I?
Breezy:	She doesn't wear anything around the house.
Host:	What do you mean, she doesn't wear anything around the house?
Breezy:	She goes around without her clothes on. Buck naked. Naked as a jaybird. When she answers the door she grabs a towel. It's disgusting, but the guys love it.
Host:	Ah, uh, uh, let's take a break.

The show lasts an hour. Other mothers and daughters are seated on the stage during the commercial breaks. They are encouraged to express their reasons for being jealous of their mothers. Among the complaints are: "She never wears a bra," "She always has her blouse unbuttoned so you can see almost down to her belly button," "My mom wears short skirts, then crosses her legs so that her underpants show." "She practices sexy smiles in front of a mirror, then smiles that way at my boyfriend."

By the end of the program forty-six members of the audience have given advice. All the mothers and daughters have said they loved each other and did not want to stop going out together. Each daughter wanted her mother to change, each mother said she would not.

Most families are not like "The Cosby Show" and never were like the reruns of "Family Ties," "The Brady Bunch," or "Father Knows Best." The girls that appeared on the talk show long for "the perfect mother." They daydream about what a mother should be like. They hope for change. It's not going to happen. The mothers are just as jealous of their daughters. They dress as they do because they long to be young and vibrant. That's not going to happen either. The obvious truth is that teenage girls—tall, short, thin, or overweight—all have something in common: They are young. Most young people have tight skin, strong teeth, and infectious laughter. They have enthusiasm, energy, vitality, sparkle, and spunk. These mothers and daughters could grow and become stronger people if they sought counseling.

Author Leo Buscaglia gets to the point when he suggests: "Never idealize others. They will never live up to your expectations. Don't overanalyze your relationships. Stop playing games. A growing relationship can only be nurtured by genuineness." The Breezys of the world need to take Buscaglia's words to heart. They also need to realize that what's going on between them and their parent is called role reversal: The teenager has become the adult in the relationship.

Dwight's Experience

Dwight, a high school student, and his sister, Joy, a seventh-grader, have a good relationship, but it was not always that way. As a little boy Dwight had always wanted a brother or sister. He was five years old when his mother and father adopted a little girl. Everyone was excited when they went to the hospital to get the child and take her home. Dwight heard someone say she was special because she was "chosen" and the parents didn't have to take a baby because it was born to them. That bothered Dwight, but he didn't know why. Years later, he remembered how he had felt upon hearing that Joy was special: He had felt jealous.

Everyone said how lucky Dwight was to be a big brother now. The baby had curly hair, and Dwight thought she was pretty for such a tiny thing. In the beginning he liked her a lot. The problem was that she had colic and was always crying. It seemed to Dwight that Mom and Dad were always rocking her or walking the floor with her. Dwight felt he wasn't getting his share of attention. Somehow he wasn't so sure he liked having a little sister. He didn't know why everything about her seemed to be wrong. He also didn't know why he had started to wet his bed at night.

One day something happened and all that changed. Joy had been crying nonstop for what seemed hours when Mom suddenly turned to him and said. "I don't blame you for not liking your baby sister. I tell you, son, there are times when I don't like her either." Dwight remembers how he felt at that moment: He was shocked. Nevertheless, it was a good thing to know and think about.

Dwight's expectations of a sister did not include someone red-faced, squalling, and attention-grabbing. Whether his bed-wetting was a way to get his parent's attention or a nervous reaction is not known for sure. However, his mother's outburst validated his feelings, and as Joy's colic lessened, his parents seemed to have more time for him. Another good thing was that he stopped wetting his bed.

When Dwight was seven he took his baby sister to school for Show and Tell. "This is Joy," he told the class. "She is a very good little sister." Now almost eighteen, Dwight still considers Joy, at thirteen, a darn good sister.

Expectations

By the simple fact that we are part of a family, we are constantly subjected to both positive and negative emotions. The way we deal daily with anger, hostility, trust, suspicion, honesty, deceit, guilt, envy, and jealousy can make a difference in the kind of person we become. If we live in a family where abuse is a common practice, a dysfunctional family will result. Adverse behavior is commonly accepted and passed on. Even when a person is aware that family life is out of focus, it's difficult to change things.

If we live in a family where trust and self-worth are priorities, the chances are we will learn to cope with most of our problems. It's also easy to take the good life for granted and be critical of others whose situations are less fortunate.

Rule No. 6. Realize That Life Is Not Always Fair.

CHAPTER ◇ 8

The Legacy

Being motivated, adaptable, and resourceful, having certain skills and abilities, are qualities that may have been bequeathed to us by our parents. In turn, these traits were passed on by predecessors. In the same way, tendencies toward greed, laziness, and inefficiency are probably handed down. "You can't tell Chandra a secret," Zoe says. "She blabs everything." Zoe is unaware that Chandra's grandmother and mother have reputations as gossips; Chandra appears to be carrying on the tradition.

The way we handle money is passed on to us by our parents, who inherited the skill or lack of skill from their parents, our grandparents. Studies show that behavior such as incest, violence between siblings, and emotional and physical child abuse is often transferred from one generation to the next.

Career choices, much like Tante Elise's bunt cake recipe, are passed along from one generation to the next. Gary Karr has been called "the greatest living virtuoso on the double bass." It is a fact that he is a seventh-generation bassist. Appreciation for the rich dark music of the double bass originated with Gary's great, great, great, great grandfather. It is not uncommon for families, decade after decade, to earn their livings as teachers, nurses, farmers, shopkeepers, or tradesmen. Religion, ethics, and politics are commonly handed down, as are attitudes. Curt says he's going to vote Republican when he is old enough to vote. "Why not Democratic?" someone asks. "Well," Curt answers, "I come from a long line of Republicans."

As a rule we don't mull over the things we have learned from our family ties; they are ingrained and settled in habit. They could be deeds that are good or bad, foolish or prudent, useful or a waste of time. In Diane's family the mother darns the socks; in Perry's family brown sugar is used instead of white; in Bill's family only tea is served. Diane's, Perry's, and Bill's explanations are simple: "That's what Grandma or Grandpa did."

In Ben's family it is important to buy Ford cars. Grandpa Wiseman does this, and so does Ben's father. "We only have Fords in our family," says Ben, "because a long time ago Grandpa Wiseman's father worked at the Ford plant in Dearborn. He always said a Ford was the very best. It's fun to get together with Grandpa, Dad, and the uncles and talk about cars." When asked if Escorts and Pintos could compare with foreign cars, his answer was, "In our family no one would consider anything but a Ford. Next year I'll be looking around for a secondhand car. It will be a Ford, of course."

The Mixed-up Mrs. M.

Mrs. Muddle and her daughter were preparing dinner. Mrs. Muddle took a large roast from the refrigerator and cut off the end. Then she put the roast in a big pan and placed it in the oven. "Mom," her daughter said, "I notice that you always cut off a large piece of the roast before you put it in the oven. Why is that?"

"I do it because it's the way my mother, your grandmother, prepares roast beef," Mrs. Muddle answered.

The next time the young girl saw her grandmother, she asked, "When you prepare a roast, why do you always cut off a large piece?"

"Ah," replied the grandmother, "I do that because I buy a large roast and my roasting pan is small."

BREAKING A CYCLE

Sometimes parents fail because they are human; tensions happen and problems arise. But there's a vast difference between facing everyday hurdles and living in a dysfunctional family. Not everyone receives the gifts of affection, regard, and respect from parents. If our parents are loving, generous, and caring, good self-esteem will enable us to handle negative emotions as we grow and develop. Without that nurturing, coping with life's woes is not easy. Everyone is born with a touch of envy, and some of us develop a knack for displaying it freely. If young people see adults acting out envy and jealousy, their inborn temperament is reinforced and the behavior is condoned.

It is a fallacy of the worst kind to say that people cannot change. People cannot change other people; people *can* change themselves—if they want to. Separating the wheat from the chaff means learning what is good or bad for us. The first step in making a change in bad habits is to recognize that the behavior is, for whatever reason, unacceptable. Next, sort through memories and try to relive feelings. Then start making changes. It won't be easy, but it can be done. If you come from a family in which anger, revenge, and jealousy rage, a change in your attitude may be necessary for you to have a normal and productive future.

Cal

Cal and his father, Doug, are great friends. They go fishing and to baseball games in the summer. In the winter they ride their snowmobile. Each year they plan a special weekend skiing at Vail. They have done this as long as Cal can remember.

Cal recalls, "The other day Dad and I got to talking, and he said the darndest thing. 'Cal,' he says, 'we go fishing, skiing, and take in ball games together. We have good times. Son, how often do you think I did this with my dad?' 'Probably every weekend, like we do,' I said. 'No Cal, that's not the way it was. My dad was a fine man. We worked a lot together and he rarely said a cross word, but we never had any fun. Your grandfather was a stern man, and so was his father. I always wanted something different for my son.'"

Doug has been successful in breaking a cycle. In all probability, Cal and his future children will have a closer and more gratifying relationship.

BRAIN POWER

The brain is divided into two parts; the left side controls the right side of the body, and the right side of the brain controls the left side of the body. Emotions seem to be centered in the right side, or hemisphere. That wonderful organ receives, remembers, and stores information. It perceives relationships and associations. It separates fact from fiction, the literal from the figurative. It is a fact that we forget more than 80 percent of the data we learn, hear, or are given. Nevertheless, it is all stored there waiting to be used, often in the form of memories.

The Memory File

William Wordsworth, a 19th-century English poet, called memory "that inward eye." Shakespeare called it "the warder of the brain." Cicero, a Roman orator, politician, and philosopher, referred to memory as "the treasury and guardian of all things." The Irish author and wit Oscar Wilde used tender words in describing it as "the diary that we all carry about with us."

Some memories are happy and some are hard and ugly. When the right button is pushed, all sorts of images and feelings can be triggered. Good or bad, memories are tucked away in the brain, and it takes only a nudge to bring them to the surface. Reaction to a long forgotten event can be reevoked by hearing laughter, a particular song or a joke, by seeing a face in a crowd, by smelling something baking. For Carl, seeing a small boy cry was all it took to awaken a long-buried memory.

Carl

At the mall, Carl noticed a mother and a small boy. The child had tripped and fallen, and the mother comforted him. She patted him, kissed his cheek, and wiped away his tears. Carl stood frozen, wondering why he had suddenly felt a terrible sorrow wrap itself around him.

"For some reason I was jealous of that kid. I didn't

even know who he was, but I felt this overwhelming resentment because he was getting something I wanted. For an instant I had been the little guy with the bunched-up face crying his heart out. As that mother took care of her little boy, I remembered how good my mom had been to me. She died when I was about five. All of a sudden I couldn't catch my breath, and I felt like crying. I sat on a bench and thought about it. Then I realized, 'Hey, wait a minute, this is actually a good feeling.' For a split second I had been that boy, and his mom had been my mother. I had experienced something long forgotten; call it a flashback or memory, whatever. Sitting there I actually began to feel happy."

Memories, like people, have shapes and with the years can change. As time goes by, people reflect on their childhood home, friends, school days, groups and clubs that they joined. They remember their parents, brothers and sisters. Cousins, so important in childhood, are apt to lose significance to adults. The past, too, has a way of changing from what we remember. Sometimes that is good. A humorous memory becomes more comical and more fun to relate. It is easy to embroider something that happened to us long ago.

Bert

"Kids don't understand that it's important to know how to deal with jealousy. I believe parents are responsible for that. They don't explain what it can lead to. Parents are supposed to teach their kids right from wrong and how to act. It's the same with lots of things. They tell you stuff like don't pick scabs and be sure to cut your toenails straight across, but they skip explaining that picking a scab can cause infection and if you don't cut your toenails right it can cause sore toes. I hate to say it, but I was sixteen before I figured that out. I think parents waste a lot of time nagging instead of giving reasons."

GENERATIONAL HABITS

A great deal of our behavior, such as family tradition, is handed down to us by our forefathers. The way we celebrate birthdays and holidays falls in that category. All of us inherit "gifts" from our ancestors. It may be the gift of easy laughter, the innate desire to aid those in trouble, the talent to sew a fine seam, the skill to use a saw, play the piano by ear, or even spell any word you hear.

Emotions, too, are inherited. "That family has always been argumentative," someone will say, or "Education has always been a priority with the Smiths." The way we worship is a legacy. In different societies customs vary as to how the dead are mourned. When Fred's grandfather died, mourners met at his house to toast his life. Fred's friend Jason said, "If this were my family, they would be crying, falling all over one another, and anxious to read his will. That's the way it is in any family funeral I've gone to. Everyone wants to know how much money was left." How people around us cope with bad situations makes a difference in our lives. It can even make a difference in the lives of generations to come.

Memories about Jealousy

Keeping up with the Joneses means having more or better possessions than a neighbor, friend, or relative. Only when that is accomplished are the feelings of envy satisfied—until the next time. Dissatisfaction with being and having less than the finest is often a characteristic originated by those who came before us and continued by immediate family members. Only when we begin to understand the negative aspects of jealousy are we able to come to terms with it. How anger, hurt, envy, and jealousy are confronted in your family was probably learned from your ancestors. Your ability to make changes in your life may depend on how problems were handled one, two, three, even more generations ago.

Some common jealous attitudes that often come down from one generation to the next are the following:

- Rich people are snobs.
- Smart kids are geeks.
- Football players are jocks.
- Alcoholics and fat people are weak-willed.
- People on welfare or public assistance are lazy.
- Cheerleaders are stuck on themselves.

If traced back, these things were probably said long ago by someone trying to bolster his or her own self-esteem.

Sometimes problems of jealousy are resolved by events in our lives that we never considered. That's what happened to Estella Rodriguez and Bea Singer, who go to the same high school but are not acquainted. They have both been involved in hurtful situations of jealousy that were resolved in completely surprising ways.

Estella

"My cousin, Sinfo Rodriguez, came to the States three years ago. He enrolled in junior high. I liked

Sinfo and so did our cousins, but we all thought he had serious problems: He was fat as an elephant, and he spoke English poorly. Everyone made fun of him because he couldn't even order a pizza or a Coke. He felt dumb and miserable. He was so unhappy he dropped out of school and got into trouble. We all felt sorry for Sinfo but had little patience. He had this great opportunity to live in the United States and get an education, and he was acting like a fool. It was a terrible worry for everyone in the family. You have to understand that we all need to stick together because we are trying to be successful in a new country. Sinfo was the only one that was a problem. His parents cried, our uncles hollered at him, and our aunts were constantly running to the church to light candles and pray.

"Finally his father sent him back to Mexico. I saw Sinfo last year, and he's now in the 11th grade and doing well. Has he ever changed! He grew tall, thin, and handsome. Sinfo said to me, 'Estella, you have no idea what rage I felt in America. I did not fit in. I was jealous of everyone. It gnawed at me every day, and I was being chewed up. I was only fourteen years old, and I felt like dirt. That's wrong, Estella.' I think my cousin was right in going back to Mexico."

Bea

"Last year when my best friend suddenly died I was devastated. We had gone to school together all our lives. We talked about how much we liked being sophomores and how much better it was than in junior high. Desira was so beautiful. After her death I was filled with guilt. I had always been jealous of her figure. Sometimes I would eat candy and brownies in front of her to tempt her into having sweets. That was mean. I regret it. To ease my conscience, I recently went to see her mother and told her about my jealousy. Desira's mom was so sweet. She said, 'I had the same feelings, dear. Desira was such a skinny Minnie. When I was her age I was tiny, too, although I may not look it now. Sometimes I begrudged the fact that she was young and pretty and had such a beautiful figure.' After that we cried together."

Rule No. 8. Find Ways to Handle It.

CHAPTER 9

What It's All About

I t is hard to conceal jealousy. People may admit their hateful feelings, but it isn't easy. Boys and girls who concede that they are often jealous say that their friends considered them so.

Teenage Jealousies

- Romance: boyfriends/girlfriends
- Looks: hair/complexion
- Clothing: figure/physique
- Popularity: being cool/having humor
- Family relationships: best friends/buddies
- Attention and recognition
- Independence and power
- Money and life-style
- Talent and accomplishments
- Being allowed to own pets

THE INTENSITY OF FEELINGS

Probably the most common feeling of jealousy is the fleeting twinge upon seeing a friend or relative with something that you've wanted for a long time. It could be designer jeans or a leather jacket, or even something less costly like a sweat suit or leggings. You've seen a leather jacket at the mall or drooled over it in a catalog. Then you see a chum wearing that very garment. For a moment you feel a stab of disappointment. "That traitor," you think, but you are able to handle it. You may say, "Hey, nice jacket," and mean it. Well, almost.

It may be more difficult to cope with envy when the desired object centers around achievements and accomplishments. You have worked your buns off to be in the marching band, practiced your instrument for hours to make first chair, but have been passed over. Someone else was chosen. It is only natural to feel hurt and jealous. No one likes to be considered not as good as the next person. When Inga, a sophomore, did not get the much-desired violin first chair in the orchestra, she was so angry and jealous that she refused to congratulate the honored player. As everyone applauded the senior boy who had won the position, Inga stomped off in a snit.

Inga said later that she felt as if she had been hit in the face. Only after the conductor talked to her did she calm down. He pointed out that she had two more years of school and could very well be first chair by her senior year. "The envy was a bad feeling," Inga said, "like someone reminding me every few minutes that I wasn't good enough. The feeling went away after Mr. Henley talked with me. Now I'm mortified about how I acted."

VIOLENCE

An eleven-year-old girl bit off two toes of her new baby sister. Obviously there were many reasons for this appalling situation, but it is also clear that the deed was the result of anger, malice, resentment, and jealousy. Violent acts such as beating, crippling, maiming, and slashing have been in the news in recent years. Occasionally jealousy ends in murder. A famous crime of passion involved Jean Harris, the headmistress of a boarding school for girls in Virginia. Jean Harris loved Herman Tarnower, a doctor who specialized in cardiology and internal medicine and was the author of several popular diet books, among them *The Scarsdale Diet*. When Dr. Tarnower turned to another woman, Jean Harris shot and killed him. The prosecution called the case "jealousy pure and simple," and Ms. Harris was sentenced to twenty years in prison.

It is interesting to note that in a 1976 survey of 143 murders, only 20 were committed by women. Of course, outrageous and shocking cases do occur. A recent example of murderous rage caused by jealousy happened in the small city of Channelview, Texas. According to newspaper accounts, it involved two attractive women, Wanda Holloway and Verna Heath, and their fourteen-year-old daughters, Shanna Holloway and Amber Heath. The families had been neighbors for nine years, and Shanna and Amber had attended the same elementary school before starting junior high.

The trouble began when both girls tried out for the cheerleader squad, and Amber was chosen but Shanna was not. The following year Wanda Holloway tried to help Shanna win a spot on the squad by getting her pencils and rulers imprinted with her name to hand out while campaigning for votes. Verna Heath objected to the school board, and Shanna was disqualified from the tryouts for violating a rule forbidding handouts.

Shanna's failure to make the squad had a maddening effect on her mother. Mrs Holloway was known in the town for her social ambitions. Shanna was doubtless disappointed, but her mother was not about to ignore this supposed rebuff.

Wanda Holloway called her former brother-in-law, Terry Harper, and proposed that he kill both of the Heaths. The price settled on was $7,500. Later, meeting with Harper, Wanda decided she could afford only getting rid of Verna. He was either to kill Verna or kidnap her and ship her to another country to be sold into white slavery. Wanda rationalized that Amber would be so upset over her mother's death or disappearance that she would be unable to continue as a cheerleader. Shanna could then take her place on the squad.

What Wanda didn't know was that Harper was working with the police. During his talks with Wanda he wore a concealed wire, and their conversations were taped. In 1991 Wanda Holloway was indicted for solicitation of capital murder.

This account of jealous rage is so bizarre that it would not be credible in a novel or a movie. Nonetheless the case points up an important truth: Never underestimate jealousy. Uncontrolled, jealousy is an overwhelming force that can result in dishonor, disgrace, and ruined lives.

People never grow too old for romance, nor too old for jealousy. Young or old, jealousy can lead people to outrageously silly acts such as spying, reading someone's diary, or calling on the phone to "check up." All too often a jealous person's retaliation against a loved one and a real or imagined adversary is absurd, even funny.

The Coach

Shelly and Chuck had been married for six years and had two children. Chuck was a popular high school coach. At

times Shelly felt envious of people with careers. Sometimes she was jealous because women, teachers and
students, seemed to enjoy being around Chuck, but she
tried to keep her negative feelings to a minimum. Once,
however, she found a package of condoms in Chuck's
blazer pocket and suspected he was having an affair with
one of his coworkers.

Chuck was out of town on a basketball trip, so Shelly
couldn't confront him. She cried a lot and had a sleepless
night. She even considered filing for divorce, but Chuck
was a good father and had always been a terrific husband,
at least until then. Later Shelly calmed down and decided
to get even. She wrapped the condom package in Scotch
tape, decorated it with Halloween stickers, and replaced
it in the jacket pocket. She was even able to laugh a bit as
she thought of how frustrated Chuck would be the next
time he met with his lady love.

When her husband returned home, Shelly had little to
say. At dinner Chuck didn't seem to notice. He was excited
because the team had won the big game, but eventually
his conversation turned to other things. "You know," he
said, "last week at the teachers' meeting we discussed the
school's plan of setting up an AIDS information program
and maybe even making condoms available. My briefcase
is full of brochures, and I need to take time to look them
over." For a moment Shelly held her coffee cup in mid-air
as she realized that the "evidence" she had found was a
handout from a teachers' meeting. Saying she had some
mending to do, she gave Chuck a warm embrace and
headed for the bedroom to remove the evidence of her
jealousy.

The Perfect Couple

Another boy-girl relationship that can be surrounded with jealousy is the school's perfect couple. Boys and girls have paired off as long as there have been high schools. Over the years couple relationships have been described as "an item," "going steady," "hangin' out," "hangin' in," "close," and "tight." In every school there is invariably a couple that everyone admires and wishes they could emulate. On the other hand, it is hard not to be envious, too. This jealousy is probably less intense than that felt when a boy or girl is "dropped" or "dumped" for someone else, but more powerful than when something material is the object of envy.

Classmates admire yet envy the perfect couple. He is a Golden Boy, tall, tan, and on the football, basketball, and track teams. She is a Golden Girl, bubbly, with perfect teeth, is in the theater group and on the pep squad. Together, as they walk arm in arm, they look adorable. Sometimes you see them at their lockers talking, laughing, maybe even kissing. You approve of them; after all, they are friendly and cheerful. Like everyone else, you admire them and absolutely know they have wonderful times and will love each other forever. They not only do their homework together but they shop at the mall on Saturday, watch all the Sunday football games at his place, and share pizza at least twice a week. You are positive that their folks approve. Without a curfew, they can probably be together as much as they want.

It's not that you're exactly jealous, and it's not as if you don't have a romantic interest of your own. Perhaps he or she is someone you see at school and have a major crush on, or maybe it's someone that you've known forever and see every day. Maybe it's someone you consider a steady, but your parents never allow you to date on school nights. When you even mention that you have a "steady," your parents may act like they are coming unglued. You're sure that the perfect couple's parents would never act like that.

Shooting Down the Myths

Remember, this is all in your mind. This is your fantasy about the perfect couple. You don't actually know that they spend a lot of time at the mall, although you may have seen them there once or twice. Maybe they watch Sunday football games together, but chances are that three or four of Golden Boy's buddies are there, too, and Golden Girl is bored out of her mind. They may share pizzas, but probably the tab, too. Most teenagers have part-time jobs these days, which cuts down on the socializing. Parents may indeed approve of their child's boyfriend or girlfriend, especially when good grades show that their studying together pays off. As for the loving couple's not having a curfew, forget it. Because of America's serious drug and alcohol problems, most parents have rules and set limits. Chances are the perfect couple in your mind live by much the same rules your parents set.

A lot of your romantic ideas are the product of your imagination. Television, magazines, and movies tell us that Madonna is the Material Girl and can have anything and anyone she wants, Michael Jackson can have anything money can buy, and beautiful Liz, owner of the Hope diamond, can have it all, has had it all, and still wants more. Bruce Willis and Demi Moore, Melanie Griffith and Don Johnson are Hollywood's perfect couples, wearing wonderful clothes and jewelry, driving classy cars, and living in fantastic houses. Of course, they're happy. Aren't they always smiling, smiling, smiling. You're right, they are beautiful people, but remember that selling their beautiful image is their job. Because you see the perfect couple almost daily, it's easy to put them in the same category as the famous people we see on television and in the movies. Anything you read about the stars invariably includes the words handsome, beautiful, and talented, the same words used by you and everyone else when talking about the perfect couple. What you have to keep in mind is that the image that is being projected by these glamorous people is not always reality.

To young people, everything appears to center on their needs and wants. "Life is a bowl of cherries" and "The world is my oyster" are sayings that surely were written for the young. However, as boys and girls mature and experience life in the adult world, their ideas and viewpoints invariably change. That does not always happen to rock, movie, and television stars. Because of the adulation and mega-buck life-style, they often get out of focus. Idolized men and women who believe their own PR can easily get stuck in a time warp of their golden selves, unable to develop normally. Multiple marriages, estranged children, battles with alcohol and drugs, and lost fortunes are all too common among the rich and famous who do not have the inner core of strength called common sense. The secret is to realize that there's life after high school and that one needs to take time to reevaluate personal and social values.

Some Facts

The problem of jealousy has not been studied to a great extent, but some facts are obvious:

- It doesn't take much to stir up jealousy in a jealous person.
- A tie exists between romantic jealousy and self-esteem.
- Jealous people are unhappy people.

In our society, male economic success and female physical attractiveness are prized. In actuality, beautiful girls may have the worst of it. Invariably, beauty breeds jealousy and envy between boys and girls, but even more so between girls and girls. In spite of this obstacle, however, beauty and power go together. Girls may protest, but it's unlikely that many would choose anthing else over being attractive. Priorities for most teenagers include looks, hair, friends, school, and a car. In a survey of forty-nine boys and girls, they ranked the factors that they felt would help them most: stress management 56 percent, self-esteem 50 percent, and resentment and forgiveness 42 percent.

Rule No. 9. Never Underestimate Jealousy.

CHAPTER ◇ 10

The Classroom

Everyone likes Mrs. Martin's Human Relations and Behavior Class. It is an elective course for 12th-graders at Thomas Jefferson County High School. The class meets three times a week, and topics are introduced by Mrs. Martin with suggestions from the students. With her encouragement, the issue is discussed and ideas are written on the chalkboard. Time is allowed for the students to write their personal thoughts in their journals. Toward the end of the period students volunteer to read what they have written.

Some of the topics for discussion have been emotional and heart-wrenching for many of the students. Alcoholic parents, family violence, suicide, sexual abuse, and AIDS have touched the lives of most of the young people.

ROOM 108

On Monday morning the boys and girls were glad to see their friends after Christmas vacation. When Mrs. Martin announced in class that the week's subject would be jealousy, it caught the students' interest. "We had millions of relatives visit for the holidays, and I saw a lot of what might be considered jealousy," someone said.

"Most of us feel good during holidays, especially when we have families to celebrate with," Mrs. Martin said. "On the other hand, it can be a time of stress. People tend to overdo, or maybe they spend too much money on gifts, or eat and drink too much. When people are burned out or have worries, it's easy to say or do what they normally wouldn't. It's easy to hurt feelings or have feelings hurt when we work or play under pressure."

"I get it," another student said. "It's like there's so much to do and so little time to get it done. It's easy to gripe when things don't go your way."

"Right," Mrs. Martin said, "so let's begin by talking about the feelings of jealousy. When you are jealous, how do you feel?"

After a moment's consideration, the kids called out "mean," "crushed," "abused," "put down," and "sickening."

"Exactly," Mrs. Martin said, writing the words on the board. "Let's go into more detail."

The students came up with the following:

- "It's this sick feeling you get when you see some-one with something you want."
- "It involves a person who is unsure of himself and tries to find fault in someone else."
- "It is something that makes you feel angry. It could be money, or looks, or life-style that someone else has. You think you are 'entitled'."
- "It's a very hard pain in your mind and gut. It just eats away your soul."
- "Jealousy is begrudging someone a success or an

accomplishment. It could be a personality characteristic like a sense of humor."
- "It is wishing you had something that belongs to
someone else. It could be anything from hair to an
outgoing personality."
- "It's the feeling of inadequacy brought on by com-
paring one thing to another."
- "Jealousy is what I feel with them winning and me
losing."
- "It has a lot to do with loving someone."
- "Jealousy in my mind has everything to do with the
girl I hang out with. It's the feeling I have when
she looks past me at some other guy."

Everyone agreed that the definitions seemed to cover
the subject. The students moved into groups to talk about
it before writing in their journals. Before the period
ended there was time for several to share their thoughts
by reading aloud.

Max

"Jealousy is a very natural human emotion which
is easily triggered by a classmate's, colleague's, or
friend's success in school, work, or relationships.
When this happens you may have a quick rush of
envy and want to be in that person's shoes instead
of your own. It can become obsessive when your
thoughts dwell on the issue. A hatred of that person
can result. The guy who can get beyond the momen-
tary pang can probably even be happy for the other's
success."

Mia

"I feel that jealousy is wanting something that you can't have. Maybe someone close owns something wonderful or can do something better, like ice skating or even leg lifts. I think it results from feelings of insecurity or inferiority. I used to feel jealous when my ex-boyfriend paid attention to other girls, because I wondered what they had that I didn't. I thought about it a lot, and now I know. Him. I guess Joe Romeo wasn't really much interested in me, but it took me a while to catch on."

Peg

"It's the feeling I have when I wish I were in someone else's place. With me, that happens a lot. It's not the wish . . . it's the feeling. Desire for a change is associated with it, and it can lead to strong dissatisfaction with one's own situation. I know, because I fight this a lot."

Before the bell rang, Mrs. Martin said, "Someone mentioned that they had a lot of visiting relatives at holiday time. They said they saw behavior that could be considered jealousy. Would that person like to comment on what happened?"

"That was me," said Wes. "We had Christmas dinner at Grandma's. I sat by Aunt Ethel, and she made remarks about Grandma's cooking: The turkey was dry, the potatoes were lumpy, and there was no green vegetable. She kept complaining. Frankly, I was glad, because it left more room for pie, and Grandma makes great pies. I think Aunt Ethel is jealous of my grandmother, who is her mother-in-law. Everyone brags on Grandma's cooking, and Aunt Ethel can't stand it."

"That's probably not an uncommon situation in a lot of families," Mrs. Martin said. "At our next class we'll talk about it."

Wednesday

"Do you ever get jealous of someone in your family?" Mrs. Martin asked. Everyone groaned. "It's called sibling rivalry," someone said.

When Mrs. Martin asked for examples, hands flew in the air.

"I'd like to go first if no one cares," Chloe said. "I'm really mad, and I'm not going to take it anymore."

"I can see you're upset," Mrs. Martin said. "We all want to hear what you have to say, Chloe, but try to calm down a little."

Chloe

"I am 5'2" and weigh 165 pounds. At one time I lost 25 pounds and looked great. My sister, on the other hand, is 5'7", weighs 105 pounds, and wears size 5. She's thin like our father, and I'm heavy like our mother. Anytime I bring a boy home, he falls in love with her. Guys are always talking about how beautiful she is. I have to live with that, and I am fed up. My sister wants to look like a model, and she does. If I show a picture of her to friends they invariably say, 'What happened to you?' Sometimes people call us Laurel and Hardy. It hurts.

"I see my sister every day. I love her dearly, but sibling rivalry is different from rivalry with a friend.

Once I went to Weight Watchers, and my sister went with me. She wore black spandex pants and a black sweater. I was embarrassed when she told the leader that she felt fat and wanted to lose weight. When she asked me to go to aerobics, I was jealous because she had the energy and the motivation to go. Not me. I feel worthless with this puffed-up body, and when my sister says she feels fat it makes me furious.

"Sometimes she starves herself to lose weight, but most of the time she can eat anything she likes. She eats candy bars in front of me all of the time.

"In our family I'm the fat one and she's the skinny one. People always say, 'Your sister looks great, but you have the pretty face,' then they add, 'If you weren't so big, you'd be the prettiest.' People also say things like, 'Beauty is from within,' and, 'Fat people laugh and are outgoing.' It's probably true because they are trying to make up for being fat.

"Mom feels bad about all the fighting, and I know I'm as obsessed with weight as my sister is. I need to learn discipline and moderation, but that's easier said than done. Everyone around me makes me feel guilty about my weight, and I just get more and more jealous."

"You're certainly honest," said Mrs. Martin. "Well, class, what about it? Any ideas?"

Everyone had an idea. The suggestions ranged from "Ignore it" to "Why not lose the weight?" When Charlie Braver said, "Hey, you look terrific to me," Chloe was obviously pleased.

Brad had a theory. "I'm convinced that a man's priorities are different from a woman's. For example, men don't worry about their weight as much as women do. I'm probably the runt of the family. I'm 5'11" and buy my clothes off the rack. My brothers are much taller and have to go to specialty shops. It's no big deal. Men have different kinds of problems and are more concerned with their careers and sports than spending much time with weight problems and being jealous of how other guys look. Not that men don't get too heavy, too fat. It all boils down to priorities."

"Okay," the teacher said. "I don't know how much we've helped you, Chloe, but at least you got your feelings out in the open."

"That is what I like about this class," Wes said. "Everyone gets a chance to express their thoughts."

"I want to hear everyone's story," Mrs. Martin said," so let's move into a circle for more informal discussion. You go first, Wes, then we'll go around the circle and talk about our feelings about jealousy."

"I picture jealousy as an ugly green monster that sneaks up on you like something from outer space," Wes said, and laughed. "It's destructive. It promotes lack of confidence. If a person feels that a lover, friend, or family member is giving them good reason to be jealous, then it's a whole different matter. There could be a more serious problem lurking there. Like with my Aunt Ethel. She's not only jealous of my grandmother; she's probably jealous of a lot of other people."

"Yes, you're right," Mrs. Martin said, "but keep in mind that some people enjoy misery. It's hard to believe that for some it's a way of life, and they don't want to change it. Now I have another question for you. Do you ever get jealous of other people in your immediate family?"

"My stepsister, she gets all the ante, perks, prizes."

"Sure, my brother, because he's a butthead."

"It's called sibling rivalry."

"Being the youngest of four kids, my brothers and sisters were jealous of me getting more than they did growing up."

"Yes, I felt that my mother loved my sister more. I never forgave Mom for giving her my doll. I loved that doll. I laugh about it now, but it still hurts."

"One of my sisters was jealous of everyone else, but at different times. To me, it always seemed like she just wanted to be treated equitably—not more, just the same. She was jealous of our older brothers' and sisters' freedom to stay up late and play with neighborhood friends. It's understandable, because as a younger sister I felt that way, too."

"We all got along very well and spent pretty much even amounts of time with each other. Occasionally, my little brother would get jealous when I got something new, or vice versa, but it rarely lasted more than a few minutes."

"There was almost no jealousy among members of my family. My mother would sometimes get mad at Dad for spending too much time at work. However, I didn't see that as jealousy. I saw it as valid anger, because he was and still is a workaholic."

"For a large family, I don't believe ours has an over-abundance of jealousy. Our parents value fairness and equity. When we were younger, any feelings of jealousy seemed to come out at Christmas if someone got some-thing the others wanted. On the whole, we are always proud of any member's accomplishments. Sometimes there are pangs of 'I wish I was that good at something,' but I think we are mostly glad to be related to that successful person!"

"Sure, I found myself jealous of my older brother and sisters because they were close in age and were able to do a lot with each other. They had so much fun that didn't include me."

"Yes, I felt my older brother was always favored over my sister and me. It's understandable, because he's a good person and everyone's favorite. He jokes and laughs a lot. I'm not sure I'm jealous of him. I think I want to be like him."

"My stepbrother was jealous of my higher grades."

"No, nothing more than the usual sibling rivalry. My sister has always seemed to be my parents' pet and to get more time and money. I guess I don't like it, but I can't do anything about it."

Stacia was the last to speak. "I am the oldest child," she said carefully. "I believe at times my younger sister was jealous, but I did not recognize it. As we entered high school I became jealous of her ease in making friends, finding time for fun, and having a steady boyfriend. This is hard to admit, but it was sort of like turn about is fair play."

Mrs. Martin then suggested that the students write in their journals about the most outstanding or worst example of jealousy in their family. "Does it have to be about sibling rivalry?" Wes asked. "I don't have brothers or sisters."

"Okay," Mrs. Martin said, "write about any situation in your life, not necessarily in your family, that concerns jealousy. Let's say it doesn't need to be anything in the past; it can be something going on right now."

After working for a while, several students volunteered to read what they had written. The following examples are short stories about jealousy written by boys and girls in Mrs. Martin's class.

"I have grown up in the wealthy part of town, but my family is not rich. Most of my friends have more money than I, and they don't have part-time jobs. My life has been comfortable, but I get jealous when my friends' parents buy them cars or trucks without a second thought. I get jealous of the good stuff my friends have. I try to remember that owning 'things' isn't the really important part of life, but it's not easy."

"The most overwhelming feelings of jealousy I have ever experienced concerned a guy I was dating. I was madly in love with him, and he knew it. I have never felt so enraged and hurt as I did when he went on another date and let me know about it. I think he was deliberately trying to make me jealous. It worked. I cried for days. He asked me to go with him again, and I really wanted to, but something held me back. Maybe it was pride. I still think about him and wish things could have been different. I am embarrassed about how I carried on."

"I was jealous when my brother got old enough to do what I did. I also was jealous of all the activities he became involved in, which included a broader range than I was allowed. By the time he was older, there was more money in the family. He could afford to join groups and get into activities that were too expensive for me when I was his age."

"Sometimes I become very close to a girl and then she gets a boyfriend. I find myself becoming jealous of the time she spends with the guy. Mom says this is natural, and that when I have a boyfriend I'll spend all my time with him. Since she told me that, I try to be more considerate of girlfriends when I'm going with someone."

"I am envious and angry because certain groups have advantages over other groups. I am jealous of males that have more advantages than females, of white males that have more advantages than minorities, and of adults that can lord it over children. I think this is jealousy, but it may be anger."

"I remember, as a freshman, feeling so jealous of a friend who did well in a talent competition. She's really a nice person, and I feel ashamed of myself now."

Friday

"It's hard to admit that we could ever have mean thoughts about our friends," Mrs. Martin said. "No one wants to admit that they let jealousy and envy creep into their lives. However, it is part of life, and how we cope with our feelings is what counts. As we all know, to cope means to struggle or contend with solving a problem, and there's no escaping problems. The saying, 'If it isn't one thing, it's another,' is only too true. Sometimes we take on challenges that are not ours, and that leads to real trouble. It's called not minding our own business. We need to learn how to back off from problems we don't own. The truth is, in this world there's plenty of trouble to go around.

"Problems involve doubt, uncertainty, and difficulty. How we work at solving them depends on how seriously they affect us. Certainly problems vary in seriousness. Sometimes when we're faced with a dilemma we try to ignore it and hope it will go away. That doesn't happen very often."

Cori spoke up. "I would like to talk about the problem of jealousy when it comes to dating. I don't always cope well with jealousy. When I feel jealous of someone—it's usually a girl after my boyfriend—I try to act unhurt and untouched. I do things to 'get him back' like making telephone calls, writing notes, and even having a party and inviting him. It doesn't always work; in fact, it's usually a waste of time. If a guy is interested, he's interested, and playing games is pointless. I try to work on my self-confidence. I know if I were more confident I wouldn't do a lot of the ridiculous stuff I do."

Everyone in the class agreed with Cori that the strongest feelings of jealousy result from getting "dumped" or having another person cut in on a relationship.

"I only wish I were wiser when it comes to men," Cori added. "It seems I'm always getting hurt."

"Maybe now would be a good time to talk about how to end a relationship that, because of jealousy, is not good for you," Mrs. Martin said.

"It makes sense to me," Cori said. "Frankly, I need all the help I can get."

"It seems to me that you've taken the first step," Mrs. Martin said. "You know that you have a problem, and you want to do something about it."

Mrs. Martin is wonderfully insightful at helping her class learn to cope. She is teaching the boys and girls that the first step in solving their problems is admitting them and then making a serious effort to resolve them. When it comes to finding solutions for problems, most of us are like Cori and need all the help we can get.

Cause and Effect

Nothing in life—anger, anxiety, distrust, jealousy—is so well fixed that one can put a finger on the exact cause and the cure. The key is to think about it and work it out. Ask yourself:

1. The cause—why did the situation occur?
2. The effect—what are the results or reactions?

You feel stress when you are confronted with a new or demanding situation. For teenage boys and girls the common **causes** of stress are school, peer pressure, grades, appearance, death or divorce in the family, family relationships, part-time jobs, decisions about the future, and the breakup of a romance.

The **effects** of stress may include an outbreak of acne, lack of energy, sleeplessness, inability to concentrate, overeating or loss of appetite, depression, and irritability.

You can evaluate the link between stressful situations and their possible consequences by understanding the cause and effect. Sometimes we focus on either cause or effect. You may read an article about why a teenager's romance ended; that would concern causes. Another article may discuss the problems that follow a romantic breakup; that would be effect. There are several ways to approach problem-solving. How you go about it is up to you. Systems that work for others include:

1. Seeking help from an adult.
2. Making a list of pros and cons.
3. Reading self-help books.

Rule No. 10. Start Fixing Yourself.

CHAPTER ◇ 11

Trying to Stay Sane

Everyone agrees that an ounce of prevention is worth a pound of cure. In other words, preventive medicine for any kind of illness or behavior is better than the worry, time, effort, and energy required to solve the problem. The best strategy, before jealousy and envy invade your life, is to try to prevent its happening in the first place. Jealousy is a complex emotion that is felt more strongly by some than others. Some people cause more jealousy than they experience. Boys and girls who want to be together as a couple can lessen the chance for jealousy by discussing, in the beginning, what kinds of behavior they can and cannot tolerate in a relationship. Of course, it's not easy, but keep in mind that an ounce of prevention is worth . . .

Know Your Own Mind

Sierra is thirteen and a freshman in junior high. She says that sometimes there is peer pressure to try alcohol and drugs, but she's against it. Her parents do not allow her to date, and that is okay with Sierra. She does not plan to date until she is old enough to make what she calls reasonable decisions in a unsafe world. "Goals are important to me and my parents. It's a good way to live," she says.

"When kids my age go together, it usually means they pay their own way to the skating rink. Sometimes they meet at a movie or a basketball game. In science class there's a boy named Mickey Monday. We talk and laugh a lot together. I like him, and you could say I have a crush. Not long ago another guy in the class asked if I would hang out with him. When I told him I wasn't interested, he got mad. I know he is jealous of Mickey. Later the guy egged and T.P'd my house."

Revenge

Probably the most overwhelming jealousy arises from a breakup of a relationship. Sometimes people need to take responsibility for behavior that may provoke others to act in a negative way. If they have the insight to suspect themselves of generating jealousy, it would be wise to explore their habits and ask themselves a few specific questions: Do you intentionally make your love interest jealous? Do you flirt with others to irritate him or her? Do you deliberately induce jealousy to see how he or she will react? Making someone jealous to stay in control of a romance is a shallow tactic. Disaster is the certain result.

Being Dumped

It's hard to take the affront of being dumped or dropped. If it happens to you, it's important to know that it's human nature to be curious about the competition, what the rival looks and acts like. Accomplishing this mission with grace is important, because your self-respect and dignity are at stake. Refusing to let go, insisting that things can be fixed is not reasonable. It only aggravates the situation and prolongs the heartache. When jealousy and possessiveness pass for love, it is not attachment, caring, and commitment; it's a sickness.

A Little Goes a Long Way

It is natural to feel betrayed if someone takes over your boyfriend or girlfriend. You are bound to feel left out, hurt, and humiliated. Dwelling on jealousy can lead to crying spells, depression, and physical illness. Sometimes anger and the feeling of having been double-crossed makes you crave revenge. You might deliberately ignore, slight, or ostracize the person. Pulling a face or giving the cold shoulder to the former sweetheart or newfound love are other forms of retaliation. Such conduct, while self-defeating, is fairly harmless.

On the other hand, disaster is certain when a rejected person is obsessed with getting even. Playing mean and cruel pranks is not uncommon for jealous and off-centered people. A sick strategy is sitting in a car to keep tabs on him or her. Other retaliatory behavior might be the twisting of truth, malicious gossip, hate mail, incessant telephone calls, trashing a school locker, ganging up, and even inciting fights. People only delude themselves if they think that such behavior will solve the problem of a romantic triangle. Revenge only intensifies anger and jealousy.

GETTING OUT

You've been in a relationship for a number of months. At first it was wonderful. You went places together, laughed a lot, and were proud to show him or her off to your friends. You were assured of a date at all school functions, and having a boyfriend or girlfriend gave you status among your peers. Best of all, your parents approved. Everything was perfect, when somewhere along the way something hit a snag. When jealousy arose you tried to ignore it. Then you felt it must be your fault and tried harder to make the relationship work. When you neglected your studies and friends, you felt twinges of guilt. Your self-esteem started to take a beating, and that wasn't normal for you. You bent over backwards to say and do all the right things. You were kinder, gave more compliments, listened more attentively. For a while you noticed that you were giving most of your time, thought, and energy to making that other person happy. You have always been willing to give more than fifty percent to any friendship, but here you were, giving eighty percent or more. You knew something was wrong, but what? After a while his or her tantrums and your anger got old. You finally said to yourself, "Who needs it?" Still, breaking off a relationship is hard to do.

For many reasons, it's difficult to put an end to romance. The person you've been involved with has become a part of your life. Being together is a habit. It has given you security, which is a grand feeling. Most important of all, you love the person. At least you think you do.

As time goes by, you become aware that your concentration is being constantly interrupted by anxiety. Movies of the two of you keep running through your head. Your love seems not to trust you, sometimes not even to like you, and that hurts. You think about how it was and how it is now.

After weeks of sleepless nights, you decide you have to do something to resolve your distress. You decide to take an inventory of your innermost thoughts. The first step is to write down all the things you admire and respect about the person: He or she has a great sense of humor, is a good athlete, works hard at school, and seems well liked by others. Then you write down all the things you do not admire or respect: He or she is late a lot; talks about other people who are always calling on the phone; complains that you should do something with your hair, that your clothes aren't right, that you should lose weight or build muscle, that you should read more important books and your driving is terrible. When you got a new camera for Christmas, he or she didn't have much to say about it—nor when you made the honor roll or were voted most likely to succeed. What you found out by this exercise was that the person's good qualities were the short list! Still, because you have a fear of abandonment, being alone, you try not to make waves.

Examine the Situation

Another thing that hit you between the eyes was that the person you have cared so much about and considered closest in your life—was jealous. You were stunned, but why else talk about other guys/girls calling all the time; complain about your hair, clothes, weight; criticize the books you read and the way you drive.

You felt bad when he or she wasn't impressed with the new camera, but you were truly hurt when your top grades weren't mentioned and the special honor you were given by fellow students was ignored. Hey, you tell yourself, something is wrong. Slowly it dawns on you that you are in a destructive relationship. For a moment you fast-forward your life, and you don't like the what you see.

For someone to be jealous when you are doing your

best to please doesn't make sense. Yet, there it is in black and white, if you can believe your own writing. The question is, what do you do next?

Get with the Program

It's a waste of time to argue about jealousy. Ideally, the thing to do is to talk it out. Tell him or her what you like, find charming, adore, and love. Next, the showdown. Ask why he or she feels the need to put you down, and itemize the things that have hurt you. The answer is getting clearer all the time. He or she is jealous. You hate to mention it because it sounds so petty. It is petty, but you've gotten through the rough part and kept your self-respect. Or have you? Has the discussion merely brought on more criticism, accusations, anger, and hurt. It might be a good place to call a halt, say good-bye. The time is now, you tell yourself. But backing off from a relationship is never easy.

Ending a Relationship

There are effective ways to deal with jealousy. Whether someone is jealous of you or you find yourself feeling jealous more than you care to admit, it's time to take responsibility for yourself. The steps are:

1. Self-reliance. Keep a tight rein on your expressions of sadness, anger, or embarrassment. Remember, there's always someone thinner and prettier, taller and more handsome. That's the way it is in the real world.
2. Positive comparisons. Think about your good

qualities. Do something nice for yourself. Bolster yourself-confidence.

3. Selective ignoring. Decide that the person is not that important. Seek another interest. The world is full of cute girls and great guys.

THE PHENOMENON OF SISTERS

The problems of jealousy and envy are not always easily and quickly resolved; sometimes it takes weeks, months, and even years. An interesting illustration is the relationship between sisters.

As children, sisters feel the emotion of jealousy when they believe that one receives more attention than the other. They retaliate by tormenting and insulting each other. As teenagers they vie for the attention of the same boys and fight about clothes. As sisters mature, their envy may take a different form. They may compare engagement rings, weddings, houses, cars, and vacations. As the sisters' children grow, their accomplishments are weighed and measured against one another. As time passes, however, a remarkable phenomenon comes to pass: In old age most sisters become best friends and often live together. The bond between them is stronger than anything else in their lives.

TIME PASSES

It is mysterious how the long green finger of jealousy can reach into the past. It can tap a shoulder, elicit a nervous giggle, and rouse a memory. With most people minor situations that happened years ago can be embarrassing to talk about. The following stories were told by Luella,

Andrew, Mavis, Mitchell, and Elizabeth, "senior citizens" who regret their jealous behavior of half a century ago.

Luella

"I lived in a convent school as a young girl, but I was not too sad when the nuns told me I didn't fit in and asked me to leave. Returning home on the bus, my seatmate was a girl my age. I was glad to know that she lived on a neighboring farm, for now I had a new friend. She was so pretty. She had beautiful blonde hair that lay in ringlets about her face. I, on the other hand, was dark with plain brown hair. Even though I admired my friend, I was jealous. I decided that if our coloring were more alike I would feel happier. I suggested that we tint our hair red like the actress Clara Bow, a famous flapper in the 1920s. My friend agreed. At the drugstore I bought the coloring, which was called henna. My friend came to my house and we went out in back, past the goat barn, chicken coops, and cob shed, where there was a small building used for butchering. Here there was a table for our supplies and we could get water from a hose that I pulled through the fence. We followed the directions, making a paste of the henna, then rubbed it into our hair. My heavy, coarse hair resisted the dye and didn't change color. My friend's fine, fair hair easily absorbed the dye and turned ruby red. When her parents saw her, they were shocked and furious. I didn't admit that it was my idea and that I had tried to henna my hair, too. In my heart I felt good that my friend looked ridiculous."

Andrew

"When we were youngsters my brother and I didn't get along. Wilfred was a big kid, strong, healthy, and mature for an adolescent boy. I was the runt of the family. I played the violin, sang in the church choir, and always had my nose in a book. I wanted to be like Wilfred, but for health reasons there was no way. Wilfred was always calling me names like shrimp, or bones, or mama's boy. He bullied me a lot, but no one knew about that.

When my brother was seventeen he was a Golden Gloves boxing champion. Everyone in our farming community admired him. He was always bragging about being the champ; in fact he acted a lot like Muhammad Ali. Once the townspeople had a parade for him, with flags, a marching band, and a banner with THE CHAMP scrawled across it. I was overcome with envy. I refused to go to the parade, and while everyone was out I trashed Wilfred's room, put rocks and sticks in his bed, and threw his school books in the nearby creek. It was foolish of me, of course; for one thing, when he found out what I had done he started to beat the whey out of me. It was pure accident that during the scrap a clock fell from the bureau, hit Wilfred on the head, and knocked him cold. As he was coming around I told him I had landed the blow. He was embarrassed to think that a scrawny kid could punch him out, and he made me promise never to tell what had happened. I've never admitted the lie I told sixty, seventy years ago. Now we are old men. In the summer we fish together and in the winter we sit in the park and play chess, but for some reason he never brags when he catches the biggest fish or beats me at chess."

Mavis

"During my high school years I lived in a town of 4,000 people. A bunch of us became leaders. We had fun at slumber parties, trading clothes, and meeting at the Malt Shoppe. Once we decided to bleach our bangs. We used peroxide and Ivory soap. It took courage. In those days no one did fashion highlights or frosting. At school another group of girls reported us to the principal. They were probably jealous, because they did something really spiteful. They said we were a sex gang and bleached bangs was our emblem. Each of us was called into the principal's office and asked to explain. I was so ashamed I didn't know what to say. I was devastated by the principal's questions and thought I was branded for life. I knew I could never tell my parents. I didn't know what a sex gang was then, and I don't know what a sex gang is now."

Mitchell

"When I was a youngster my family were poor, my mother chased off her husbands, and my brothers often refused to go to school. It was depression days. Welfare programs had names like PWA, WPA, and CCC. My family was on relief. To help out, I delivered papers in the Heights, the ritzy part of town. I knew some of the kids who lived there; we all went to the same high school. I remember being filled with envy. Sometimes as I walked through that part of town I was angry and bitter because those kids had so much and I had so little. At some point I decided to turn things around. Jealousy pushed me to succeed. It could have had the opposite effect, of

course; it would have been easy to become a drop-
out. Instead, I worked at getting good grades,
applied for scholarships and loans, got through university and eventually earned a Ph.D. Recently I
gave a lecture at a national meeting of American
Social Workers. Its title was, 'How It Feels to Be in
the Welfare System and Get Yourself Out.' I stressed
that there are feelings you have to remove from your
life, especially envy and jealousy. It's a hard way to
go. Learning to cope is of utmost importance."

Elizabeth

"My best friend in junior high was Willa Mae Scott.
She had long, thick, wonderful tresses while I had
a thin, dishwater-blonde mop of hair. I convinced
Willa Mae that her hair and mine would look better
in a bob. We agreed to have our hair cut over the
weekend. Willa had hers cut, but I didn't. Further-
more, I had never intended to do so. I had been
mean and sneaky because I was jealous. Willa Mae
took the whole thing well, even ignoring the fact that
I had backed out on our bargain. No doubt she had
much better self-esteem than I. Besides, she looked
great with short hair."

RULES HELP

You can chew yourself up with jealousy or take steps to
learn how to cope. When you feel envious or jealous you
need to be realistic, think rationally about what the problem is, then get to work on resolving your feelings. You
need to have control of your life. Coping with jealousy is

like taking an onion apart. First remove the papery covering and then the tough layer. After that it becomes easier, even with tears.

Rule No. 1.   Identify your feelings.
Rule No. 2.   Stay calm.
Rule No. 3.   Know that learned behavior can be unlearned.
Rule No. 4.   Develop insight.
Rule No. 5.   Talk about feelings.
Rule No. 6.   Learn to cope, cope, cope.
Rule No. 7.   Realize that life is not always fair.
Rule No. 8.   Find ways to handle it.
Rule No. 9.   Never underestimate jealousy.
Rule No. 10. Start fixing yourself.
Rule No. 11. Have control of your life.

For Further Reading

NONFICTION

Arnold, Eric H., and Loeb, Jeffery, ed. *I'm Telling! Kids Talk about Brothers and Sisters*. New York: Little Brown, 1987.

Cohen, Daniel and Susan. *Teenage Competition, A Survival Guide*. New York: M. Evans, 1986.

Gaylin, Willard, M.D. *Feelings, Our Vital Signs*. New York: Harper and Row, Publishers, Inc., 1979.

Harris, Thomas H., MD. *I'm O.K.—You're O.K.* New York: Avon, 1986.

Schoenfeld, Eugene, M.D. *Jealousy: Taming the Green-Eyed Monster*. New York: Holt, Rinehart and Winston, 1980.

Tavris, Carol. *Anger, the Misunderstood Emotion*. New York: Simon and Schuster, 1982.

Winthrop, Elizabeth. *A Little Demonstration of Affection*. New York: Harper and Row, 1975.

FICTION

Andrews, V.C. *Flowers in the Attic, Petals on the Wind, If There Be Thorns, Seeds of Yesterday, Garden of Shadows*. New York: Pocket Books division of Simon and Shuster Inc., 1984–1992.

Anthony, Evelyn. *Anne Boleyn*. New York: Thomas Y. Crowell, 1957.

Banks, Lynne R. *Indian in the Cupboard*. New York: Doubleday, 1980.

Bates, Betty. *Picking Up Pieces*. New York: Holliday House, 1981.

Bronte, Emily. *Wuthering Heights*. New York: Macmillan, 1963.

Conford, Ellen. *Lenny Kandell, Smart Aleck*. New York: Little Brown and Co., 1983.

Du Maurier, Daphne, *Rebecca*. New York: Doubleday, 1938.

Hinton, S.E. *Ramble Fish*. New York: Delacorte, 1975.

———. *The Outsiders*. New York: Viking Press, 1967.

Lowry, Lois. *A Summer to Die*. New York: Bantam, 1979.

Michael, Judith. *Deceptions*. New York: Poseidon Books, 1989.

———. *Inheritance*. New York: St. Martin's Press, 1989.

Miller, Marcia. *Jealous Yesterday*. New York: Avalon Books, 1967.

O'Dell, Scott. *Island of the Blue Dolphins*. New York: Dell, 1987.

Paterson, Katherine. *Jacob Have I Loved*. New York: Thomas Y. Crowell, 1980.

Rackin, Phyllis. *Shakespeare's Tragedies*. New York: Um. Ungar, 1978.

Rock, Gail. *Addie and the King of Hearts*. New York: Bantam Books, 1976.

Rubens, Bernice. *I Sent a Letter to My Love*. New York: St. Martin's Press, 1978.

Sachs, Marilyn. *Fourteen*. New York: E.P. Dutton, 1983.

———. *Fran Ellen's House*. New York: E.P. Dutton, 1987.

———. *Just Like a Friend*. New York: Dutton, 1987.

———. *Baby Sister*. New York: Dutton, 1986.

———. *The Fat Girl*. New York: Dutton, 1984.

Shakespeare, William. *Romeo and Juliet*. New York: Gramercy Books, 1990.

Sharmat, Marjorie. *I Saw Him First*. New York: Dell Publishing Co. Inc., 1983.

White, T.H. *The Sword in the Stone*. New York: Putmam Publishing Group, 1939.

Zindel, Paul. *Effects of Gamma Rays on Man-in-the-Moon Marigolds*. New York: Harper, 1984.

————. *The Girl Who Wanted a Boy*. New York: Bantam, 1985.

————. *Confessions of a Teenage Baboon*. New York: Harper and Row, 1977.

Index

A

accomplishments, jealousy of,
30, 62, 64–65, 68, 77–78,
104–105, 114–115, 123
advertisements
influence of, 33, 52–54
subliminal, 51
AIDS (acquired
immunodeficiency
syndrome), 47, 108
anger, 2, 13, 18, 21, 25, 32, 35,
37–38, 47, 57, 93, 97, 101,
102, 106, 114
anxiety, 5, 47
apologies, 14–15, 18
attention, jealousy of, 29, 104
avarice, 37–38

B

behavior
changing, 96–97
inherited tendency to, 25–26
nervous, 21
patterns of, 30–31
unacceptable, 15, 57
betrayal, feeling of, 2–3, 128
birth order, of siblings, 37
bitterness, 1, 57

bond
between mother and child, 30
between sisters, 132
Brown, H. Jackson, 21–22
Buscaglia, Leo, 91

C

child abuse, 56–57, 94
Cicero, 98
counselor
family, 51
school, 38
stress management, 29
covetousness, 4, 6, 36, 38
crimes of jealousy, 12, 106–107
cultures, jealousy in, 32

D

deadly sins, seven, 37–38
despair, 3, 47, 60
divorce, 1, 65, 82
rate, 40, 47
drug/alcohol abuse, 47, 51, 111

E

emotional disturbance, serious
(SED), 56

emotions
  excessive, 60
  inherited, 100–101
  mixed, 93
  negative, 25
envy, 4–7, 21, 37–38, 93, 101
expectations
  family, 46–47, 93
  over-high, 91
  teenage, 67, 78

F
family
  dysfunctional, 93, 96–97
  jealousy of, 62–63
  jealousy within, 113–114,
    116–117
  and sibling rivalry, 37, 45,
    46–49
  violence, 49–51
fear, 1, 2–3, 25
feelings
  awareness of, 26
  identifying, 2
folk tales, jealousy in, 20
Freud, Anna, 23–24
Freud, Sigmund, 22–24
friendship, jealousy in, 2, 10,
    36, 61–62, 68, 78, 122–123
  sibling, 40

G
Glasser, William, 29
gluttony, 37–38
greed, 20, 21, 38
Grimm, Jacob and Wilhelm, 20
group therapy, 58
guilt, 24, 32, 34, 38, 65, 68, 93,
    102, 129

H
hard sell, in advertising, 54
Harris, Jean, 106–107
hatred, 18–19, 20, 24, 32, 34
Holloway, Heath case, 106–107
hurt feelings, 1, 11, 33, 70, 101,
    105, 130

I
independence, jealousy of, 64,
    104
insight, 54–55, 60

J
jealousy
  classroom studies of, 113–125
  definitions of, 1–15, 34,
    114–116
  difference from envy, 4–5
  feelings of, 114–115
  handling, 16–17, 20–22,
    37–38, 30, 37, 39, 52,
    67–67, 77–81, 99–100,
    123–124
  kinds of, 7–15
  in literature, 18–20
  memories about, 100–103
  mother/daughter, 84–91
  motivations for, 29–30
  stories about, 61–63,
    121–123

K
Klein, Melanie, 24

L
Life's Little Instruction Book,
    21–23
life-style, differences in, 63–67

looks, jealousy of, 30, 104, 112,
    117
love
    in family, 37
    in folk tales, 20
    genuine, 36
    need for, in infancy, 24
lust, 37–38

M
manipulation, of others, 35, 68,
    75
memories of childhood, 59,
    132–136
memory, 25, 98
money, jealousy of, 58, 78–79,
    104, 112
Mozart, Wolfgang Amadeus, 19

N
names, importance of, 23,
    70–73
neglect, child, 57
newborn sibling, jealousy of,
    7–9, 26–28, 42–44,
    75–75, 105–106
nicknames, 71

O
obsession, envy as, 5
ostracism, 38, 128
ownership, jealousy of, 29

P
parents
    exploitative, 56–57
    and sibling rivalry, 44–46
    structured, 47–48
Pendley, Darrell W., 29–39

perfect couple, jealousy of,
    109–111
play therapy, 24
popularity, jealousy of, 66, 104
prevention, as coping skill,
    34–35, 126
pride, 37–38
professional jealousy, 7, 10–11,
    79–81
psychiatrist, 22
psychoanalysis, 22–24
psychologist, 16, 22, 38
    point of view of, 29–39

Q
qualities, inherited, 94–97

R
relationship
    boy-girl, 109–111
    ending, 124–125, 128–132
    family, 82, 97
    jealousy of, 66, 98–99, 104
    sibling, 40, 44
    stepfamily, 91–93
    unhealthy, 36
revenge, 12, 14, 97, 127, 128
role-playing, 39
role reversal, 91

S
Salieri, Antonio, 19
self, acceptance of, 34–35
self-esteem, 3, 16, 24, 30, 97,
    101, 129
selfishness, 38
    versus jealousy, 31
sexual jealousy, 7, 12–15
Shakespeare, William, 18, 98

shunning, 38
sibling
  envy, 5–6
  jealousy, 7–9, 62, 122
  rivalry, 36–37, 40–55,
    117–118, 119–121
Silverstein, Shel, 19
sixth sense, 54–55
social jealousy, 7, 9–10,
  106–107
Sophocles, 19
stepfamilies, jealousy in, 83–84
stress, cause and effect, 125
superstition, 19–20

T
tantrum, 32, 50–51, 75
Tarnower, Herman, 106

television
  influence of, 51–54, 110–111
  talk shows, 82–93
traditions, family, 100–101

V
Verdi, Giuseppe, 18
violence, 1, 12, 105–107
  family, 49–51
  sibling, 40–41, 94

W
Wilde, Oscar, 98
Winterset Home, 56–69
Wordsworth, William, 98